THE LAST GAME

How the world almost ended over Kashmir

Col Alok Asthana

ISBN – 978-93-343-5211-5

Preface

This book is a dramatized account of an actual conflict between India and Pakistan during May 2025. Most of the conflict took place broadly in this manner, but not exactly. To that extent, it is to be treated as fiction, not history.

The "72 Hour War", as this conflict is also known as, remains one of the closest approaches to nuclear exchange since the Cuban Missile Crisis, and serves as a stark reminder that in an age of nuclear weapons and rapid technological change, small conflicts between regional powers can quickly threaten global civilization. The crisis also demonstrated how technology transfer relationships can fundamentally alter regional strategic balances in ways that challenge traditional approaches to strategic planning, intelligence assessment, and crisis management.

I have studied this conflict extensively and have written three books on it – each with a different twist, for a different reader. The first two books provide the data and reasons. My first book on it – **Op Sindoor – Force Multipliers and Dividers: What worked and what did not** – is a data-driven technical analysis where data is presented mostly in the form of tables with some explanations. The researcher will find it invaluable. The other book – **Strategic leverage; The novel about how Op Sindoor got checkmated** – presents the facts that gave rise to the data, but as dialogues between diplomats, former generals, intelligence officers, and journalists from across South Asia, participating in a

3 day seminar. much after the war. That format greatly facilitates assimilation of facts. This third book is a proper novel. It is not at all about data, but the story.

This is meant for the reader who would enjoy a techno-thriller novel, with all its fast moving action and the thrill of war. Here, you'll get all you got from *The Sum of All Fears* by Tom Clancy, and more. That was pure imagination. This is mostly reality.

Prologue

May 4, 2025 - 3:30 PM
Intelligence Bureau Field Office, Srinagar

Inspector Rajesh Khurana stared at the intelligence report he'd been drafting for two days, knowing it would likely disappear into the bureaucratic maze that had paralyzed India's security apparatus. The document outlined suspicious activities around known terrorist hideouts: unusual movement patterns, encrypted communications using sophisticated protocols, financial transfers through previously unknown networks.

Everything pointed to a major operation being planned.

"Sir," his deputy, Sub-Inspector Sushmita, entered carrying another file. "The intercepts from yesterday show increased chatter about 'the pilgrimage season.' They're definitely planning something targeting in Kashmir."

Khurana rubbed his temples. At 45, he'd spent twenty-three years in intelligence, watching bureaucratic caution consistently override operational urgency. "Priority assessment?"

"Imminent threat level, sir. I'd say 72-hour window maximum."

"Draft it as immediate action required. Route it through proper channels but also send an informal heads-up to all station chiefs along the pilgrimage routes."

What neither officer knew was that similar warnings were being filed simultaneously across multiple agencies—RAW had financial intelligence about unusual funding flows, Military Intelligence had communication intercepts, the NSA had technical intelligence about equipment procurements. But nobody was authorized to connect the dots.

May 5, 2025 - 10:00 AM

Joint Intelligence Committee, New Delhi

The weekly JIC meeting proceeded with bureaucratic precision. Khurana's urgent assessment sat in a stack of routine reports awaiting "proper coordination" before distribution to operational commands.

"Item 47-B requires multi-agency review before field distribution," announced the JIC Secretary, stamping Khurana's warning with "PENDING COORDINATION - 72 HOUR STANDARD REVIEW CYCLE."

In Srinagar, Khurana checked his secure terminal obsessively. No acknowledgment. No questions. No action.

"Still nothing, sir," Priya reported. "Should we try unofficial channels?"

Khurana stared out at the mountains where pilgrims would soon be traveling. "Unofficial channels got people transferred to desk jobs. We follow protocol."

Protocol would cost twenty-three innocent lives.

Contents

The Pilgrimage ends

For convenience, timings throughout the book are shown in Indian Standard Time, IST, irrespective of the location of the event

May 7, 2025 - 6:15 AM
Pahalgam, Kashmir, India

Ravi Sharma had been looking forward to this day for months, checking off calendar dates and making careful preparations for what he and his wife Priya considered one of the most important journeys of their lives. The 34-year-old software engineer from Bangalore had saved up vacation days, researched the best routes and accommodations, and convinced his wife that a pilgrimage to the holy cave of Amarnath would be the perfect way to celebrate their fifth wedding anniversary while seeking blessings for the family they hoped to start.

The ancient cave, nestled high in the snow-capped Himalayas at an altitude of over 12,000 feet, drew hundreds of thousands of Hindu pilgrims each year to witness the natural ice formation revered as a manifestation of Lord Shiva. For Ravi and Priya, the pilgrimage represented more than religious obligation—it was a spiritual journey that would mark their transition from young couple to potential parents, a blessing sought from the divine before taking the next step in their lives together.

"Are you sure about this?" Priya had asked him weeks earlier as they planned the trip, scrolling through news reports about occasional security incidents and checking the latest travel advisories. "Kashmir is still... complicated. The security situation changes so quickly."

Ravi had laughed, pulling up tourist photos on his laptop showing pristine mountain landscapes, ancient temples, and groups of happy pilgrims. "Look at these mountains, these forests. It's one of the most beautiful places on Earth. And the security situation has been stable for years now. The government has really improved things, and the local economy depends on pilgrimage tourism. Everyone wants us to have a safe journey."

They had spent weeks preparing—purchasing appropriate clothing for mountain weather, arranging for time off work, coordinating with other family members who wanted to join them, and most importantly, preparing spiritually through prayer and fasting. For Priya, who came from a particularly devout family, the pilgrimage represented a lifelong dream that marriage had finally made possible.

Now, as their bus wound through the dense pine forests toward Pahalgam, the traditional base camp for the Amarnath pilgrimage, Ravi squeezed Priya's hand as they caught their first glimpse of the snow-capped peaks ahead. The morning air streaming through the partially open windows was crisp and clean, filled with the scent of pine and early morning mountain mist, carrying with it the promise of spiritual fulfillment that had drawn pilgrims to these mountains for over a thousand years.

Around them, their fellow passengers chatted excitedly about the journey ahead, creating the kind of communal anticipation that made religious pilgrimages special. The bus carried twenty-three pilgrims from across India—a perfect microcosm of the country's diversity, united by shared faith and common purpose despite differences in language, regional background, and economic status.

There was Kumari and Raman Venkatraman, an elderly couple from Chennai who had been married fifty-three years and were finally making the pilgrimage they'd dreamed of since childhood but had never been able to afford during their working years. Now, with their children successful and their own modest retirement secure, they were fulfilling a vow made in youth with the wisdom and gratitude of age.

The Gupta family from Delhi occupied the middle section of the bus—parents Suresh and Meera with their two small children, eight-year-old Anjali and six-year-old Arjun, who pressed their faces against the windows pointing at everything with the wonder that made travel magical. Suresh worked as a government accountant, and this pilgrimage represented a significant financial sacrifice, but one the family considered essential for their spiritual well-being.

Three college friends from Mumbai—Kiran, Deepak, and Sandesh—were taking a break from their final year of engineering studies to seek spiritual growth before entering the competitive world of technology careers. They occupied the back of the bus, balancing youthful excitement with genuine reverence for the sacred journey they were undertaking.

Retired Colonel Harbinder Singh and his wife Kavita were traveling from Pune, fulfilling a vow made during his service in Kashmir decades earlier when he had promised God that if he survived his military service, he would return to seek blessings at Amarnath. Now, with their children grown and his military pension providing modest security, they were honoring that decades-old commitment.

The bus driver, a local Kashmiri named Hassan Wani, navigated the winding mountain roads with the casual expertise of someone who'd made this journey thousands of times over his fifteen years of driving pilgrimage buses. His cheerful commentary about local landmarks had become as much a part of the pilgrimage experience as the destination itself, and many repeat pilgrims specifically requested his services.

Hassan took genuine pride in his role facilitating spiritual journeys, seeing himself as more than just a driver but as a guardian responsible for safely delivering devotees to their sacred destination. He knew every turn of the mountain roads, every scenic overlook worth stopping for photographs, and every local story that added meaning to the journey. His warm personality and obvious devotion to passenger safety had earned him an excellent reputation among pilgrimage organizers.

"Just ahead, you'll see the confluence of three rivers," Hassan announced over the bus's PA system, his voice warm with genuine pride in his homeland's natural beauty. "Local legend says that bathing at this spot brings good fortune for the pilgrimage ahead. We'll stop here for ten minutes so those who wish can participate in this tradition."

The passengers smiled and prepared their cameras, already reaching for small containers to collect holy water from the sacred confluence. But Hassan's attention remained focused on the road ahead, scanning for the usual checkpoint signs and security posts that marked the carefully managed pilgrimage route.

What Hassan didn't know—what none of them knew—was that seventeen kilometers away, in a safe house hidden among the pine forests, three men were making final preparations for an operation that would transform their peaceful pilgrimage into the spark that nearly ignited nuclear war between two nations.

Hamid Mir, the operation's 25-year-old leader, was a Kashmir University engineering graduate whose radicalization had been a carefully managed process extending over two years. His recruitment by The Resistance Front hadn't followed traditional patterns of religious extremism or cross-border infiltration. Instead, it had been a sophisticated operation that exploited genuine grievances while providing advanced training that suggested external technical assistance of the highest order.

"Final equipment check," Hamid announced to his two-man team as they prepared weapons and communication gear that bore the hallmarks of professional military procurement. The rocket-propelled grenades, timing devices, and encrypted communication systems exceeded anything previously seen in regional terrorist operations.

Tariq Ahmed, the team's communications specialist, had used his engineering background to develop secure communication protocols that had evaded intelligence monitoring for months. "Bus confirmed on schedule. Security posture remains relaxed due to recent improvements in cross-border relations."

The third team member, Yasir Khan, was the operational expert whose military training had been conducted not in traditional terrorist camps but in sophisticated facilities that employed methods and equipment suggesting state-level technical assistance.

"Remember," Hamid addressed his team with the calm professionalism of someone who had been thoroughly trained for this moment, "every aspect of this operation will be documented and analyzed globally. Our methods, equipment, and coordination must demonstrate capabilities that exceed expectations."

At 6:47 AM, as the pilgrimage bus rounded a sharp bend near the outskirts of Pahalgam, Hassan Wani noticed the truck positioned across the road ahead and immediately understood that his worst fears were about to be realized. But the sophistication of the ambush that followed would exceed anything he had experienced during Kashmir's most violent years.

The first rocket-propelled grenade struck the front of the bus with devastating precision, killing Hassan instantly and sending the heavy vehicle spinning off the road into a rocky ravine. The explosion shattered the front windshield and sent shrapnel ripping through the passenger compartment, but the attackers weren't finished.

The second RPG hit the fuel tank as the bus tumbled down the embankment, creating a massive fireball that could be seen for miles across the valley. The orange flames and black smoke rising from the wreckage would soon draw rescue teams, but for the twenty-three people inside, help would come too late.

The third rocket struck the main passenger compartment as it came to rest against the rocks, ensuring that no one inside would survive to tell the story of what had happened. The sophisticated attack demonstrated planning, training, and equipment that suggested far more than local extremism—this was professional terrorism with state-level support.

By the time the echoes of the explosions faded across the pristine valley, twenty-three innocent people were dead, their dreams of spiritual fulfillment transformed into a tragedy that would push two nuclear powers to the brink of war.

Kumari and Raman Venkatraman died together holding hands, their fifty-three-year marriage ending in fire with their lifelong pilgrimage dream finally within reach. The Gupta family from Delhi perished together, eight-year-old Anjali and six-year-old Arjun never understanding why their spiritual journey had ended in violence. The three engineering students from Mumbai would never complete their degrees or build the technological future they had planned.

Colonel Harbinder Singh and his wife Kavita completed their final service together, dying while fulfilling the vow he had made decades earlier as a young soldier. Ravi and Priya Sharma, whose bodies would be found holding each other in the twisted wreckage, had started the morning discussing their hopes for starting a family and seeking divine blessings for the future. Now those hopes lay buried in the burning metal of religious hatred, their anniversary pilgrimage becoming a memorial to the innocent victims of regional conflict.

The three attackers melted back into the dense forest, leaving behind a scene of devastation that would trigger military responses across South Asia. But what the world would not immediately understand was that this attack represented something far more sophisticated than traditional terrorism—it was the carefully orchestrated opening move in a strategy that would test every assumption about military technology, intelligence capabilities, nuclear deterrence, and crisis management in the modern age.

By the time Indian authorities arrived at the attack site, the narrative of what had happened was already circulating globally through carefully cultivated networks that would shape international perceptions of the crisis that was about to unfold.

Within minutes of the explosions, professionally produced video content began appearing on social media platforms that intelligence services had not identified as terrorist-affiliated.

Op Sindoor takes shape

May 7, 2025 – 8.00 AM

Prime Minister's Residence, New Delhi

Prime Minister Rajesh Patel was in the middle of his meticulously planned morning routine when his private secretary's urgent knocking shattered the carefully structured calm that began each of his days. At 58, Patel had served in various government roles for over two decades, rising through the ranks of the ruling Bharatiya Janata Party through a combination of genuine political acumen, unwavering devotion to Hindu nationalist ideology, and an almost obsessive attention to detail that had served him well in India's complex political environment.

The morning had started like every other for the past three years since becoming Prime Minister. Patel had risen at precisely 5:30 AM as was his custom, spent an hour in meditation and prayer before carefully arranged images of Hindu deities in his private temple room, and was working through his daily yoga routine when the news arrived that would transform a routine Tuesday into one of the most dangerous days in human history.

The disciplined routine that had sustained him through decades of political combat—the careful balance of spiritual practice, physical fitness, and mental preparation—now seemed pathetically inadequate to the crisis unfolding in Kashmir. But it was this same discipline that allowed him to immediately shift from personal reflection to national leadership as the gravity of the situation became clear.

"Sir, there's been a major terrorist attack in Kashmir," his private secretary announced through the door, his voice carrying the kind of controlled urgency that indicated something far beyond routine political crisis. "Twenty-three Hindu pilgrims are confirmed dead. The Home Minister and Defense Minister are requesting immediate emergency consultations."

The words hit Patel like a physical blow to his chest. Hindu pilgrims—innocent people seeking spiritual fulfillment, families on sacred journeys, devotees whose only crime was their faith—murdered by terrorists who showed no mercy for the sacred or the innocent. In his mind, he could already see the television coverage, the weeping families, the political opposition demanding immediate action, and his own party's base expecting decisive retaliation.

"How many attackers? Do we have any in custody? What's the initial assessment of responsibility?"

"Multiple attackers with sophisticated weapons, sir. Professional level coordination. All escaped. Initial reports suggest rocket-propelled grenades, military-grade explosives, and tactical coordination that indicates advanced training. The attack shows hallmarks of Lashkar-e-Taiba operations, but with significant technological enhancement."

Within an hour, Patel sat at the head of a polished mahogany conference table in the secure briefing room of the Prime Minister's Office, surrounded by his security cabinet and senior military advisors. The room itself reflected the weight of the decisions made there—portraits of India's founding fathers looking down with solemn dignity, detailed maps of the subcontinent showing both British colonial boundaries and current disputed areas, and banks of secure communication equipment that connected the Prime Minister to every corner of India's vast democracy and beyond.

Defense Minister Shantha Devi, a former army colonel with a well-earned reputation for hawkish views and tactical brilliance, spread classified photographs of the attack scene across the table. The images were horrific—twisted metal still smoking from the explosions, charred earth where the bus had burned, personal belongings scattered across the mountainside like discarded prayers, and evidence markers indicating the sophisticated weapons that had been used.

"The weapons they used were extremely sophisticated," she said, pointing to detailed forensic images of RPG fragments that intelligence teams had already begun analyzing. "This wasn't some local cell throwing stones at security forces. Someone trained these men extensively, equipped them with advanced military weapons, and provided them with detailed intelligence about the pilgrimage route, timing, and security arrangements. Someone who wanted to send a very specific message about their capabilities."

External Affairs Minister Vikram Chandra, who had spent his career building bridges between India and Pakistan through patient diplomatic engagement, shifted uncomfortably in his chair. At 61, Chandra had devoted himself to the belief that economic cooperation, cultural exchange, and generational change could eventually overcome the historical grievances that divided the two nations, but attacks like this tested his fundamental assumptions about the possibility of regional peace.

"We need to be extremely careful about making accusations without definitive proof," he said quietly, his diplomat's training evident in his measured tone. "The international community will be watching our response very carefully. If we act precipitously without clear evidence linking Pakistan's government to this attack, we could find ourselves isolated diplomatically at precisely the moment when we need international support."

"The international community?" Devi's voice rose with barely controlled anger, her military background evident in her direct approach to strategic problems. "Twenty-three innocent pilgrims are dead, Vikram. Families destroyed, children orphaned, elderly couples who saved their entire lives for this pilgrimage murdered for their faith. How many more need to die before we stop worrying about international opinion and start protecting our own people?"

"The international dimension matters precisely because this isn't happening in isolation," Chandra replied firmly, spreading his own intelligence briefings across the table. "Chinese military assistance to Pakistan has been increasing dramatically. Russian arms sales continue despite various sanctions. North Korean technical assistance has been documented. If we escalate without considering the broader strategic context and the technological assistance Pakistan has been receiving, we could find ourselves facing more than just Pakistan in any extended conflict."

But it was what came next that would define the entire crisis. Air Chief Marshal Rakesh Kumar, who had been reviewing operational plans throughout the morning, leaned forward with obvious discomfort written across his weathered face.

"Prime Minister, if we're going to discuss retaliation options, I need to address a fundamental operational issue that has significant implications for aircrew safety and mission success."

"Go ahead, Air Chief Marshal."

"Sir, our preliminary target analysis indicates that Pakistani air defenses have been significantly enhanced since our last major assessment. Standard military doctrine requires comprehensive Suppression of Enemy Air Defenses—SEAD operations—before conducting deep strike missions into heavily defended airspace."

Defense Minister Devi interrupted with barely concealed impatience. "Air Chief Marshal, we understand the operational requirements. What's your point?"

"Ma'am, my point is that SEAD operations involve attacking Pakistani radar installations, missile batteries, command centers, and communication networks. These are clearly military targets that would be interpreted internationally as acts of war against Pakistan's armed forces rather than counterterrorism operations against terrorist infrastructure."

The room fell silent as the implications became clear. Prime Minister Patel, who had been studying intelligence photographs throughout the discussion, looked up with the focused attention that characterized his approach to complex decisions.

"Air Chief Marshal, what are you recommending?"

"Sir, I'm recommending that if political guidance requires us to appear to be targeting only terrorist infrastructure rather than Pakistani military assets, we should limit operations to standoff weapons launched from Indian airspace. Sending manned aircraft into Pakistani airspace without first suppressing their air defenses violates fundamental principles of air warfare and unnecessarily risks our most valuable assets—our aircrew and our most advanced aircraft."

The military logic was unassailable, but the political considerations were equally compelling. Home Minister Rajiv Kapoor, who had been quietly reviewing domestic political assessments, spoke up with the voice of someone who understood electoral realities.

"The public doesn't want to hear about standoff weapons and technical limitations. They want to see that India has the capability and resolve to reach deep into terrorist sanctuaries when our people are murdered. The opposition is already calling for decisive action, and anything that appears cautious or limited will be interpreted as weakness."

Defense Minister Devi nodded emphatically. "The Air Chief Marshal's concerns about safety are noted, but we cannot allow operational caution to undermine strategic objectives. Our pilots are trained professionals who understand that military service involves risk."

Air Chief Marshal Kumar's jaw tightened, but his response remained professionally measured. "Ma'am, there's a difference between acceptable risk and unnecessary risk. Standard SEAD operations exist precisely to minimize aircrew losses while maximizing mission effectiveness. Skipping those procedures doesn't demonstrate resolve—it demonstrates poor military judgment."

The Prime Minister raised his hand to halt the increasingly heated exchange. "Air Chief Marshal, I understand your professional concerns. But I need you to understand the political reality we're facing. If we conduct extensive attacks on Pakistani military installations before striking terrorist camps, the international community—and particularly our own public—will see this as military aggression rather than legitimate counterterrorism."

"Sir, with all due respect, dead pilots and shot-down aircraft will be facts that no political narrative can overcome."

The tension in the room was palpable as military professionalism clashed with political necessity. National Security Advisor Ajit Singh, who had been studying the latest intelligence assessments, attempted to bridge the gap with a comprehensive threat analysis.

"Our electronic warfare capabilities should provide significant protection for our aircraft," he said, displaying technical assessments that had been prepared by the Defense Research and Development Organization. "Pakistani air defense systems, while improved, remain vulnerable to our electronic countermeasures and sophisticated jamming techniques. The risk assessment indicates acceptable casualty probabilities for operations conducted with proper electronic warfare support."

Air Chief Marshal Kumar studied the intelligence estimates with the skeptical eye of someone who had learned not to trust assessments that hadn't been tested under combat conditions. "NSA sahib, with respect, these assessments are based on theoretical capabilities and controlled testing. Combat conditions often produce results that differ significantly from laboratory projections."

"Air Chief Marshal," the Prime Minister said with finality, "I appreciate your professional concerns, but the decision has been made. We will conduct precision strikes against terrorist infrastructure in Pakistan-administered territory. Electronic warfare support will provide adequate protection for our aircraft. The political requirement is that we demonstrate both capability and restraint—striking terrorist targets without appearing to initiate broader military conflict."

"What should we announce to the nation,"

"What we must. That India will destroy the terrorist country. We don't really have to name them. Also announce that we now treat hold the Sutlej Water treaty as held in abeyance."

The decision was made in that moment, though its catastrophic implications wouldn't become clear for another eighteen hours. India would launch major air operations into Pakistani airspace without first suppressing Pakistani air defenses, not because it was militarily sound, but because political considerations required a response that appeared both bold and limited.

As the meeting concluded and participants filed out to implement decisions that would bring the subcontinent to the brink of nuclear war, Air Chief Marshal Kumar remained behind, staring at satellite photographs of Pakistani air defense installations that his pilots would have to penetrate without the standard protections that military doctrine required.

In his thirty-four years of service, including combat operations and countless training exercises, he had never been ordered to send aircrew into such unnecessary danger for political considerations that had nothing to do with military effectiveness. The decision violated every principle of responsible military leadership he had learned during decades of professional development.

But in the complex civil-military dynamics of democratic India, professional military advice could be overruled by elected leadership whenever policy objectives conflicted with operational prudence. The principle of civilian control over the military was fundamental to democratic governance, even when that control led to decisions that professional military officers considered dangerously flawed.

Outside the Prime Minister's Office, preparations began immediately for Operation Sindoor—the most ambitious Indian military operation against Pakistan since the 1971 war. But the operation would be conducted under political constraints that would transform what should have been a decisive demonstration of Indian capability into a tactical disaster that nearly triggered nuclear war.

The die was cast. Indian aircraft would fly into Pakistani airspace without the standard air defense suppression that military doctrine required, because political considerations demanded an operation that appeared restrained rather than one that was militarily sound.

In the complex calculations of democratic politics, the appearance of limitation was more important than the reality of effectiveness. Twenty-three pilgrims had died for their faith, and now Indian aircrew would risk their lives for political optics that prioritized international perception over operational success.

The failure of intelligence that had enabled the Pahalgam attack was about to be compounded by the failure of political leadership to understand the difference between appearing restrained and being strategically effective.

The announcement by the PM was made. The world started talking of an imminent war between India and Pakistan.

President Trump is told

May 7, 2025 - 11:05 AM

Somewhere over the Arabian Sea

The secure phone buzzed in the darkened cabin of Air Force One as it flew through the night sky, cutting through the humid darkness above the Arabian Sea. The aircraft's modified 747 frame hummed with the constant vibration of four massive engines pushing the most powerful leader in the world through international airspace at 40,000 feet, but the sound that mattered most was the insistent electronic chirping of the encrypted communication device on the President's nightstand.

President Donald Trump, halfway through his second term and no stranger to middle-of-the-night crisis calls, picked up the encrypted device with the practiced ease of a man who'd been woken by potential wars more times than he cared to count. At 78, Trump had thought he'd seen every possible international crisis during his time in office, but the voice on the other end of the line was about to introduce him to a new kind of strategic nightmare.

"Sir, this is General McKenzie at CENTCOM. We have a developing situation in Kashmir that requires immediate presidential attention. Twenty-three Indian pilgrims are confirmed dead in what appears to be a highly sophisticated, coordinated terrorist attack. Initial assessment suggests professional-level training and advanced weaponry. The Indians seem to be planning an attack on Pakistan."

Trump rubbed his eyes, glancing at the digital clock whose red numbers seemed to mock him with their precision. They were still six hours out from Joint Base Andrews, returning from what had been a surprisingly successful trade summit in Singapore where he'd managed to secure several bilateral agreements that would boost American exports to Southeast Asia. The meetings had run late, filled with the usual diplomatic dance of concessions and compromises, but now the careful work of economic diplomacy seemed trivial compared to the crisis erupting half a world away.

Outside the small, thick window of the presidential suite, the vast Arabian Sea stretched endlessly in the darkness, its surface invisible but somehow reassuring in its constancy. Somewhere below, fishing boats and cargo vessels went about their peaceful business, oblivious to the conversation taking place miles above them that could determine whether millions of people lived or died in the coming days.

"Terrorism or state-sponsored, General? And give me your honest assessment—I don't need political hedging at this hour."

"Too early to tell definitively, sir, but several factors suggest this goes beyond traditional terrorist capabilities. The sophistication of the attack, the precision timing, the advanced weaponry used—all of it points to professional training and possibly state-level support. The Indians are already publicly blaming Pakistan, and our signals intelligence is picking up significant military communications on both sides of the Line of Control."

"Nuclear?" The single word carried the weight of Trump's deepest fear as President—not economic collapse, not political scandal, but the possibility that his presidency might be defined by the first nuclear exchange since World War II.

"Both sides maintain significant nuclear arsenals, Mr. President. Current estimates put India at 160-170 warheads and Pakistan at 140-150. More concerning, both countries have doctrines that contemplate nuclear use under certain escalatory scenarios. We're monitoring all nuclear-related communications and facilities closely, but so far both sides appear to be maintaining normal peacetime postures."

Trump stood up in the cramped cabin, his tall frame requiring him to duck slightly under the cabin's ceiling. He walked to the window and stared out at the darkness, thinking about the weight of nuclear responsibility that he'd carried for years but had never quite gotten used to. Somewhere down there, in a region he'd visited only once and never fully understood despite countless briefings, two nuclear powers were about to engage in the most dangerous game of brinkmanship since the Cuban Missile Crisis.

The irony wasn't lost on him—he'd spent years tweeting about foreign policy, simplifying complex international relationships into 280-character statements, but now faced a crisis that could only be resolved through the most delicate kind of personal diplomacy. The kind where a misunderstood phrase or a moment of wounded pride could lead to mushroom clouds over cities filled with millions of innocent people.

"Keep me informed every one hour, General. And get me Secretary of State Rubio on a secure line as soon as possible. Also brief the Pentagon on our contingency plans for South Asian nuclear scenarios—all of them, including the ones we hope we'll never need."

"Yes, sir. Mr. President, there's one more thing. Our preliminary intelligence suggests Pakistani military capabilities may have been significantly enhanced since our last comprehensive assessment. Chinese technology transfer appears more extensive than previously understood."

The additional information created a new dimension to the crisis. Chinese involvement in Pakistan's military modernization had been a concern for years, but if Beijing's assistance had fundamentally altered the regional balance of power, traditional crisis management approaches might prove inadequate.

"What kind of enhancements are we talking about?"

"Electronic warfare capabilities that appear to approach or exceed Indian systems in certain scenarios. Advanced air defense integration. Precision missile technology with improved guidance systems. "

"Send me the DIA assessment."

The General did.

Classified Analysis - Defense Intelligence Agency

CLASSIFICATION: SECRET//NOFORN

The conventional military balance between India and Pakistan had undergone fundamental transformation since 2019.

Pakistani Electronic Warfare Revolution

The most dramatic development was comprehensive integration of advanced Chinese electronic warfare systems, creating capabilities that not only matched but in certain scenarios exceeded Indian equivalents despite lower platform numbers.

Pakistani EW assets included:

- J-10CE aircraft with Chinese EW pods capable of sophisticated jamming across multiple frequency bands
- Ground-based systems derived from Chinese Type 305A architecture
- Integrated air defense networks with Chinese YJ-12B electronic attack capabilities
- Mobile tactical EW systems at brigade level

Assessment: Pakistani EW capabilities demonstrated sophistication approaching major powers rather than regional forces.

Air Defense Integration - Quantum Leap

Pakistan's air defense network demonstrated remarkable advancement through Chinese assistance, creating multilayered coverage that significantly complicated Indian air operations:

- HQ-9B long-range SAM systems providing area defense
- FM-90 short-range systems with Chinese radar integration
- JY-27A VHF radars designed for effectiveness against reduced-RCS targets
- Integrated command using Chinese KJ-500 architecture
- Mobile SAM systems providing unprecedented flexibility

The integration level suggested Chinese assistance extending far beyond normal arms sales into comprehensive capability development.

The Crisis that never should have happened

May 7, 2025

Different locations, India

1.00 PM

Intelligence Bureau Field Office, Srinagar

Khurana sat in his emptied office, personal belongings in cardboard boxes. The transfer orders had arrived that morning: "Pending completion of internal inquiry into operational procedures."

Sub-Inspector Sushmita found him staring at his computer screen showing news coverage of the protests. "Sir, this isn't your fault. You followed proper channels."

"Proper channels got people killed, Sushmita. Twenty-three innocent people died because I was more afraid of bureaucratic consequences than terrorist attacks."

His phone buzzed with a message from his wife: *"Victim families are outside our housing complex. Security says we should stay inside."*

The intelligence failure was becoming personal for everyone involved. Officers who had tried to warn of the attack were being scapegoated while politicians who had created the dysfunctional system escaped responsibility.

"Ma'am," Sushmita's assistant knocked urgently. "There's been another development. Pakistan is releasing video footage showing their security services tried to prevent the attack but were overwhelmed by sophisticated operatives. They're claiming the real intelligence failure was failing to detect how advanced the terrorist capabilities had become."

The narrative was shifting rapidly. Pakistan was positioning itself as also being victimized by terrorism while India faced questions about competence and preparation.

3.00 PM

Research & Analysis Wing Headquarters, New Delhi

Brigadier Ranjeet Sharma stood in the sterile briefing room, staring at intelligence reports that should have prevented the Pahalgam massacre but instead had been buried under layers of bureaucratic caution and political wishful thinking. How had they missed it?

The intercepts were all there in the classified folders spread across the conference table. Unusual movement patterns around suspected training camps. Encrypted communications that used sophisticated protocols. Financial transfers through previously unknown networks. Equipment purchases that exceeded normal terrorist requirements. Everything pointed to a major operation being planned, but the intelligence community had failed to connect the dots in time.

"Sir," Major Sandhya Singh, his deputy and the most brilliant analyst he'd worked with in twenty-three years of service, entered the room carrying a steaming cup of tea and a thick file marked "IMMEDIATE ACTION REQUIRED." Her face bore the exhausted expression of someone who had spent the night reconstructing an intelligence failure that had cost twenty-three innocent lives.

"Sandhya, please tell me you've found something in the post-attack analysis that explains how we missed this."

Major Singh set down her tea and opened the file with the deliberate movements of someone delivering bad news. "Sir, we didn't miss it entirely. We had pieces of the puzzle, but they were scattered across different agencies, different classification levels, and different analytical frameworks."

She spread several documents across the table, each bearing the distinctive red stamps of various intelligence organizations. "RAW had financial intelligence about unusual funding flows. Military Intelligence had communication intercepts. IB had human intelligence about local recruitment patterns. The NSA had technical intelligence about equipment procurements."

"But nobody put it together?"

"Nobody was authorized to put it together, sir. Each agency guarded its sources and methods so carefully that comprehensive analysis became impossible. We were so concerned about preventing leaks that we prevented understanding."

Ranjeet sank into a chair, feeling the weight of institutional failure that had enabled terrorism to succeed through intelligence community dysfunction rather than terrorist sophistication. "What about the warning indicators? Surely someone flagged the unusual patterns?"

Major Singh pulled out another document, this one stamped with multiple classification markings and signature blocks. "This was drafted sixty hours ago by our technical analysis section. It identified a 73% probability of major terrorist operation within the next week, targeting pilgrimage routes in Kashmir."

"And where did it go?"

"Joint Intelligence Committee for review and coordination with other agencies before distribution to operational commands."

"When was it scheduled for distribution?"

"Tomorrow, sir. The bureaucratic coordination process takes a minimum of seventy-two hours, even for urgent assessments."

The absurdity was staggering. Intelligence analysts had correctly predicted the attack, but bureaucratic procedures had ensured that their warning would arrive twenty-four hours after the terrorists struck. Twenty-three people had died while intelligence reports sat in coordination queues waiting for administrative approval.

"There's something else, sir," Major Singh continued, her voice dropping to the tone she used for the most sensitive information. "The operational sophistication of this attack suggests capabilities that exceed traditional terrorist training. The timing, the equipment, the escape protocols—everything indicates professional military instruction."

"Pakistani intelligence services?"

"That's the obvious conclusion, but the evidence doesn't quite fit traditional patterns of ISI support. This looks more like... advanced external assistance. The kind of training and equipment that suggests state-level capabilities, but not necessarily Pakistani state capabilities."

Sharma looked up sharply. "What are you suggesting?"

"Chinese military advisors have been observed at several facilities in Pakistan-administered Kashmir over the past eighteen months. Officially, they're providing infrastructure development assistance. Unofficially, our technical intelligence suggests they may be providing advanced training in electronic warfare, communications security, and operational planning."

The implications were staggering. If Chinese military assistance had enabled terrorist groups to operate with near-state-level capabilities, the entire regional security environment had shifted in ways that Indian strategic planning hadn't anticipated.

"Sandhya, draft an immediate assessment for the Prime Minister's office. Flag this as requiring urgent strategic review at the highest levels. If Chinese assistance is creating new terrorist capabilities, the government needs to understand the implications before making response decisions."

"Sir, there's one more thing. The political guidance from South Block is that intelligence assessments suggesting Chinese involvement in terrorism are... unwelcome at the moment. The External Affairs Ministry is concerned about complicating our bilateral relationship with Beijing."

Sahrma stared at his deputy, understanding that political considerations were preventing accurate intelligence assessments from reaching decision-makers who needed them most. The same institutional caution that had delayed the warning about Pahalgam was now preventing comprehensive analysis of the strategic implications.

"Draft two assessments," he said finally. "One that follows current political guidance. Another that provides our actual professional judgment about Chinese involvement and its implications for regional security."

"And which one gets transmitted, sir?"

“Let me think. I’m having a headache right now.”

4:00 PM

Intelligence Bureau Headquarters, New Delhi

Outside the IB gates, hundreds of protesters held photographs of Pahalgam victims. "You had the warnings!" shouted Meera Gupta, whose elderly parents had died in the attack. "Where were you when our people needed protection?"

The crowd's anger was fueled by leaked WhatsApp messages showing field officers had sent urgent warnings three days before the attack—warnings buried in bureaucratic channels while officials attended routine meetings.

Inside, Additional Secretary Krishnan faced a closed-door inquiry. The evidence was damning: time-stamped intelligence reports, communication intercepts, financial tracking data—all pointing to imminent attack. All ignored.

"Explain this message," demanded the inquiry officer, reading from Krishnan's phone: "'Field assessment indicates 73% probability major terrorist operation within 96 hours targeting pilgrimage routes. Recommend immediate security enhancement and operational alerts.'"

"The message was properly channeled through JIC for coordination—"

The Leak

May 8, 2025 - 1:00 AM

Investigative Journalist's Office, New Delhi

Arjun Sharma (no relation to the victim) had been investigating intelligence failures for six months when the encrypted USB drive arrived through his mail slot with a simple note: "The families deserve the truth."

The drive contained audio recordings from the highest levels of India's intelligence apparatus:

Meeting Recording - May 4, 2025

"Field assessment indicates 73% probability major terrorist operation within 96 hours..." "These reports require JIC coordination before operational distribution..." "Coordination takes minimum seventy-two hours..." " So warnings will arrive after the attack window?" "That's... theoretically possible."

Meeting Recording - May 6, 2025 - 18 hours before attack –

"Any updates on the Kashmir threat assessment?" "Still in coordination. Should be distributed by May 8th." "What if something happens before then?" "We follow established procedures."

The most damaging recording was from May 7th morning, after the attack:

"How do we explain that we had advance warning?" "We emphasize Pakistani sophistication rather than our procedural delays." " The families are asking questions." "Redirect focus to Pakistani responsibility for the attack."

Sharma stared at the transcripts.

By afternoon, the recording would be broadcast.

VOICE 1: "We had the intelligence sixty hours in advance." VOICE 2: "Why wasn't it distributed?" VOICE 1: "Standard coordination process takes seventy-two hours minimum." VOICE 2: "So people died while bureaucrats processed paperwork?" VOICE 1: "That's... an oversimplification." VOICE 2: "Twenty-three families might disagree."

Within hours, the recordings were broadcasting on every major Indian news network and social media platform:

NDTV: "EXCLUSIVE: Intelligence recordings reveal Pahalgam attack was predicted 72 hours in advance"

Times Now: "SHOCKING AUDIO: Officials knew attack was coming but bureaucracy delayed warnings"

India Today: "THE TAPES: How red tape killed 23 pilgrims"

The leaked audio went viral internationally:

BBC: "Indian intelligence recordings suggest Kashmir attack was preventable"

CNN: "Leaked tapes show Indian officials had advance warning of terrorist attack"

Al Jazeera: "Audio reveals Indian intelligence failure contributed to pilgrimage massacre"

In the UN Security Council, the German Ambassador read from the transcripts: "These recordings suggest the tragic deaths could have been prevented through improved Indian institutional coordination rather than military action against Pakistan."

The Chinese Ambassador was more direct: "Indian intelligence failures do not justify military aggression against Pakistani sovereignty."

Even the American Ambassador seemed uncomfortable: "These revelations require comprehensive investigation before any further military escalation."

Trending hashtags:

#IntelligenceFailure - 3.2M tweets #PahalgamTruth - 2.8M tweets #StopNuclearWar - 2.1M tweets #AccountabilityNow - 1.9M tweets

Sample viral content:

@BBCBreaking: "Leaked intelligence recordings suggest Kashmir attack was preventable through better Indian coordination rather than requiring military retaliation against Pakistan" 89,000 retweets, 234,000 likes

@VictimFamily_Mumbai: "Pakistan killed our loved ones, but Indian bureaucrats helped them do it by ignoring warnings #SystemicFailure" 67,000 retweets, 189,000 likes

@AnalystDelhi: "If we had 72 hours warning and chose paperwork over people, who's really responsible for these deaths?" 45,000 retweets, 134,000 likes

@KashmirTimes: "How was there no security to stop terrorists? To harass Kashmiris, there are check posts every 2 Kms." 8000 retweets, 9000 likes

@MyKshmir: " It's Governor's rule in Kashmir. Ask him to explain." 41000 retweets. 6000 likes

The information warfare was shifting global opinion against Indian military action by highlighting preventable intelligence failures rather than Pakistani state sponsorship.

8:30 PM

Chennai, India

Krishnan Venkatesh sat in the police station, staring at forms for claiming his parents' bodies. Fifty-three years of marriage, ended together in terrorist violence. His phone buzzed with a text message from his daughter, away at university in Delhi: "Grandpa and Grandma are heroes, Dad. They died as martyrs. India will avenge them."

Heroes. Martyrs. Avenge.

The language of nationalism was already transforming his parents' deaths from a personal tragedy into a political cause. Krishnan wasn't sure how he felt about that. His parents had been quiet, religious people who avoided politics and tried to see the good in everyone. Would they have wanted their deaths to be a cause for war?

But as he looked at the forms spread before him - death certificates, compensation claims, arrangements for last rites - Krishnan found himself thinking that maybe his daughter was right. Maybe some things were worth fighting for. Maybe some attacks demanded a response.

The world discusses it

May 8, 2025 - 2:00 AM

Different locations

News Report: CNN International

Anchor Sarah Chen: "Good afternoon, I'm Sarah Chen with breaking news from Kashmir. At least twenty-three people are confirmed dead in what Indian authorities are calling a coordinated terrorist attack on a bus carrying Hindu pilgrims to a religious shrine. The attack occurred this morning near the town of Pahal gam..."

[Video: Aerial footage of the burned bus wreckage, emergency responders, crowds gathering]

"...The victims were traveling to the Amarnath cave, one of Hinduism's holiest sites, when their bus was struck by what witnesses describe as multiple rocket-propelled grenades. Indian Prime Minister Rajesh Patel has called an emergency cabinet meeting, and there are already reports of increased military activity along the India-Pakistan border."

"For analysis, I'm joined by Dr. Michael Harrison, South Asia expert at the Council on Foreign Relations. Dr. Harrison, how significant is this attack in the context of India-Pakistan relations?"

Dr. Harrison: "Sarah, this is extremely serious. The targeting of religious pilgrims represents an escalation in tactics that's designed to provoke maximum outrage in India. The Hindu nationalist government of Prime Minister Patel will be under enormous domestic pressure to respond forcefully."

Chen: "And the Pakistani response?"

Dr Harrison: "Pakistan will likely deny any involvement, as they have with previous attacks. But the sophistication described by Indian officials - coordinated RPG attacks, professional execution - suggests training and equipment beyond what local terrorist cells typically possess."

Chen: "Could this lead to military confrontation?"

Dr. Harrison: "It's possible. India has conducted surgical strikes against terrorist targets in Pakistan before, in 2016 and 2019. But both countries now have significantly more advanced military capabilities than they did then. And of course, both are nuclear powers."

Chen: "We'll continue following this developing story. When we return, international reaction to the Kashmir attack..."

The Brookings Institution, *Washington, D.C.*

May 8, 2025 - 4:00 AM IST

Emergency Panel Discussion: "Crisis in Kashmir - Implications for Regional Stability"

Dr. Susan Williams (Moderator) "Good afternoon. I'm Susan Williams from the Brookings South Asia program. We've convened this emergency panel to discuss the developing crisis in Kashmir following this morning's terrorist attack. I'm joined by three distinguished experts: Dr. Arun Prakash, former Chief of Naval Staff of India; Dr. Ayesha Siddiqa, Pakistani defense analyst; and Dr. James Patterson from the Pentagon's Defense Policy Board."

"Dr. Prakash, let's start with you. How is India likely to respond to this attack?"

Dr. Arun Prakash: "Susan, this attack represents a particularly heinous form of terrorism - targeting religious pilgrims, innocent civilians with no political or military significance. The Modi government... excuse me, the Patel government... will be under enormous pressure to respond decisively. Public opinion in India will demand action."

Dr. Williams: "What form might that action take?"

Dr. Prakash: "Most likely surgical strikes against terrorist infrastructure in Pakistan-occupied Kashmir. India has done this before, most notably after the Uri attack in 2016 and the Pulwama attack in 2019. But this time, the capabilities on both sides are significantly more advanced."

Dr. Williams: "Dr. Siddiqi, how do you assess Pakistani involvement in this attack?"

Dr. Ayesha Siddiqi: "Well, first, let me express condolences for the innocent lives lost. No political cause justifies targeting civilians. That said, Pakistan has repeatedly denied supporting terrorist organizations, and there's a difference between isolated rogue elements and state policy."

Dr. Williams: "But is that distinction meaningful in practice?"

Dr. Siddiqi: "It should be. Pakistan has made significant efforts to crack down on terrorist organizations in recent years. The problem is that when attacks like this occur, India tends to hold Pakistan responsible regardless of the evidence. That creates a dynamic where Pakistan is blamed for attacks it may not have orchestrated."

Dr. James Patterson: "If I may interject, the intelligence picture is usually more complex than either side acknowledges publicly. Terrorist organizations often have multiple sources of support, training, and financing. Attribution is difficult even with excellent intelligence."

Dr. Williams: "Dr. Patterson, what are the risks if this escalates to military confrontation?"

Dr. Patterson: "Very high. Both countries have invested heavily in military modernization since their last major confrontation in

2019. India's Rafale fighters, Pakistan's JF-17s and F-16s, both sides' missile capabilities - we're looking at a much more lethal conflict environment than existed even five years ago."

Dr. Prakash: "And of course, both sides maintain nuclear arsenals. Pakistan has adopted what they call 'full spectrum deterrence' - nuclear weapons designed to deter conventional as well as nuclear attacks. That lowers the threshold for nuclear escalation."

Dr. Siddiqi: "Pakistan's nuclear doctrine is purely defensive. We would never initiate nuclear conflict. But if Pakistan's survival is threatened by conventional attack..."

Dr. Patterson: "That's exactly the kind of ambiguity that makes this situation so dangerous. Each side has different interpretations of what constitutes an existential threat worthy of nuclear response."

Dr. Williams: "What role should the international community play?"

Dr. Prakash: "Immediate de-escalation efforts. Contact both governments, urge restraint, offer mediation services. This kind of crisis can spiral out of control very quickly."

Dr. Siddiqi: "Agreed. And importantly, any mediation needs to address the underlying issues - Kashmir, terrorism, trust-building between the two countries. Treating symptoms without addressing causes just ensures we'll be back here again."

Dr. Patterson: "The United States has particular responsibilities here. We have strategic relationships with both countries, significant influence, and frankly, the most to lose if this escalates to nuclear exchange. President Trump needs to get personally involved, immediately."

Dr. Williams: "We'll be monitoring this situation closely and will reconvene as events develop. Thank you all for joining us."

Op Sindoor takes off

May 9, 2025 - 6:45 PM

Srinagar Air Base, Kashmir

Wing Commander Arjun Singh checked his watch as he walked toward his aircraft in the gathering dusk, the approaching darkness adding an element of tactical advantage to what promised to be one of the most challenging missions of his career. The sun was beginning to set behind the magnificent mountains surrounding Srinagar, painting the sky in brilliant shades of orange and red that reminded him, with uncomfortable irony, of the fires he would soon be creating across the Line of Control.

At 31, Singh was one of the Indian Air Force's most experienced Rafale pilots, with over 1,200 hours in the sophisticated French-built fighter that now sat on the tarmac before him like a technological marvel waiting to be unleashed. The aircraft represented the cutting edge of Indian military technology—a twin-engine, multi-role fighter capable of precision strikes and air-to-air combat, equipped with some of the most advanced weapons systems, sensors, and defensive capabilities in the world.

But as Singh conducted his methodical pre-flight inspection, walking around the aircraft with the practiced eye of a pilot whose life depended on technical perfection, he was acutely aware that his technological advantages might not be as decisive as conventional wisdom and official briefings suggested. Recent intelligence reports had highlighted Pakistani acquisition of Chinese J-10CE fighters with sophisticated electronic warfare capabilities, and their air defense network had been significantly upgraded with Chinese assistance that appeared far more comprehensive than previous assessments had indicated.

Singh had grown up in a military family where service to India was considered not just a career choice but a sacred duty. His father had been an army officer who served with distinction in the 1971 war with Pakistan, and his grandfather had fought courageously in the 1965 conflict. Military service wasn't just a profession for the Singh family—it was a tradition of protecting India against those who would harm her, and each generation had built upon the sacrifices of those who came before.

"Nervous about tonight?" asked Flight Lieutenant Rahul Gupta, Singh's designated wingman, as they moved to their aircrafts.

Singh paused before answering, weighing how much of his professional concerns he could share with a junior officer. "Rahul, in all your training at the Air Force Academy and during your conversion to the Rafale, did anyone ever teach you to conduct deep strike operations against a defended target without first suppressing enemy air defenses?"

"No sir," Gupta replied immediately, his confusion evident. "That's considered fundamental doctrine—you always clear the air defense environment before sending strike aircraft into enemy airspace. Every tactical manual, every training exercise, every case study from previous conflicts emphasizes SEAD operations as essential preparation."

"And why is that doctrine considered fundamental?"

"Because unsuppressed air defenses can engage aircraft with devastating effectiveness, sir. Modern surface-to-air missile systems are designed specifically to destroy aircraft operating in their engagement zones. Sending pilots into defended airspace without suppressing those defenses is essentially... well, sir, it's essentially sending pilots on very dangerous missions with unnecessarily high casualty probabilities."

Singh nodded grimly, his worst fears confirmed by his wingman's textbook response. "That's what I thought too."

The conversation reflected a broader tension within the Indian Air Force about the operational constraints that had been imposed for political reasons. Professional military officers understood that the restrictions were designed to limit international criticism of Indian operations by avoiding attacks on clearly military targets, but they also understood that those same restrictions dramatically increased risks to aircrew and expensive aircraft.

The mission briefing had been more complex and politically sensitive than Singh had expected when he was first called to the operations center. Rather than the simple surgical strikes against terrorist camps that had characterized previous retaliatory operations, this mission had been expanded to include facilities where Chinese technical assistance was believed to be provided to anti-India militants, creating a more complex targeting scenario with potentially broader strategic implications.

"These aren't just traditional terrorist training camps," the intelligence officer had explained during the detailed mission briefing, pointing to satellite imagery that showed sophisticated facilities with advanced communications equipment and what appeared to be technical instruction areas. "They're comprehensive facilities where Chinese military advisors are systematically enhancing Pakistani proxy capabilities through advanced training, weapons provision, and operational planning support. Your mission is to eliminate not just the terrorist infrastructure, but the technology transfer relationships that are making increasingly sophisticated attacks possible."

The targeting folder had included disturbing intelligence assessments showing not just traditional training facilities with obstacle courses and firing ranges, but advanced communications equipment, electronic warfare training setups, and what appeared to be sophisticated technical instruction areas where foreign advisors were providing capabilities enhancement that went far beyond traditional arms provision.

"Sir," Gupta asked carefully, his voice dropping to the tone used for sensitive conversations in military environments, "are we expecting significant Pakistani air defense resistance?"

Singh looked at his wingman for a long moment before responding, weighing how much of his professional skepticism he should share. "Intelligence assessments suggest their capabilities are limited and that our electronic warfare systems should degrade their effectiveness substantially. But Rahul, intelligence assessments and combat reality don't always align perfectly, especially when those assessments are based on assumptions rather than recent testing."

Singh climbed into his cockpit and ran through the familiar startup procedures that had become second nature through thousands of hours of training and operational flights. The Rafale responded to his touch like a thoroughbred horse, all power and precision waiting to be unleashed in defense of India's security. Around him, five other Rafales, including that of Rahul, were preparing for the mission.

The radio crackled to life with the professional calm that characterized air force communications: "Garuda Flight, this is Control. Weather is clear with excellent visibility, winds light and variable from the northwest. You are cleared for takeoff when ready. Intelligence reports minimal enemy air activity in the target area but be advised that Pakistani electronic warfare capabilities are assessed as significantly enhanced since our previous operations in 2019. Exercise maximum caution and expect sophisticated countermeasures. Good hunting and bring everyone home safely."

As Singh's aircraft lifted off from the runway with the smooth power that made the Rafale such a pleasure to fly, he turned toward the Line of Control that had divided Kashmir between India and Pakistan for over seven decades. The mountains below were beautiful in the evening light, their snow-capped peaks catching the last rays of sunlight like natural monuments to the sublimity of creation, but Singh knew that beauty concealed generations of human conflict and continuing strategic competition.

During the flight toward Pakistani airspace, Singh thought about the pilgrims who had died that morning—innocent people seeking divine blessings, murdered by those who claimed to serve the same God. But he also thought about the larger strategic picture that the intelligence briefings had revealed: Chinese support for Pakistani terrorism, the evolving military balance in the region, and the possibility that this mission might trigger something much larger and more dangerous than the surgical strike it was intended to be.

What Singh didn't know as he flew through the darkening sky was that Pakistani radar operators, using Chinese-supplied early warning systems more sophisticated than Indian intelligence had assessed, were already tracking his formation with unprecedented precision and preparing defensive responses that would challenge everything he thought he knew about air combat in the South Asian environment.

The sophisticated air defense network that Pakistan had quietly assembled over the past four years represented far more than the sum of its individual components. Through comprehensive Chinese technical assistance and Pakistani tactical innovation, they had created an integrated defensive system that could engage advanced aircraft using methods that Indian electronic warfare systems weren't designed to counter.

But perhaps most significantly, Pakistani forces had prepared for exactly this type of Indian operation. The attack in Pahalgam had been designed to trigger precisely the kind of limited retaliation that political constraints would force India to conduct without proper air defense suppression. Every aspect of the coming engagement had been war-gamed, analyzed, and prepared for with the kind of systematic attention to detail that characterized major power military planning rather than regional defensive preparations.

Across the border, Pakistani F-16s and J-10CE fighters were being scrambled to intercept the Indian formation with electronic warfare capabilities, tactics, and coordination that would demonstrate how fundamentally the technological balance had shifted since previous conflicts. The first shots of what would become known as the "72 Hour War" were about to be fired, and the strategic assumptions underlying both sides' planning were about to be tested in ways that would reshape regional military balance for decades to come.

Singh flew toward Pakistani airspace unaware that he was about to participate in a technological demonstration that would challenge every assumption about regional military capabilities and force strategic planners worldwide to reconsider how rapidly military balances could be altered through comprehensive technology transfer and tactical innovation.

The last game between India and Pakistan was about to begin, but the rules had changed more dramatically than anyone in New Delhi realized.

First Contact

May 9, 2025 - 7:23 PM

Pakistani Airspace, 12 km inside the Line of Control

Squadron Leader Tariq Ahmed saw the Indian aircraft formation on his radar screen long before his radio operator confirmed what they both already knew from years of training and border patrol experience: "Control, Thunder Lead. Contact! Six hostile aircraft crossing the Line of Control at bearing 095, altitude 25,000 feet, speed 500 knots. Confirmed Indian Air Force penetration of Pakistani airspace."

Ahmed was flying one of Pakistan's most capable F-16 Fighting Falcons, a battle-tested American aircraft that, while not quite as advanced as the French Rafales now penetrating Pakistani airspace, had been significantly enhanced through recent upgrades and most importantly, through the integration of Chinese electronic warfare capabilities that would fundamentally alter the dynamics of this engagement.

At 29, Ahmed was a veteran of numerous missions along the volatile border with India, but this engagement felt fundamentally different from the routine patrol flights, reconnaissance missions, and occasional incursions that had characterized his previous service. The Indians weren't just probing Pakistani airspace or conducting routine border surveillance—they were coming in fast and low with obvious hostile intent, clearly planning to attack targets inside Pakistan. But this time, Pakistan was ready with capabilities that would surprise their adversaries and demonstrate how dramatically the technological balance had shifted.

"Thunder Leader, this is Control," came the calm, professional voice from the ground controller whose radar coverage had been significantly enhanced through Chinese technical assistance. "Hostile aircraft confirmed crossing into Pakistani territory. Multiple violations detected. Electronic warfare assets report successful target acquisition. You are cleared to engage if they do not respond to standard warnings. Electronic warfare support is fully active and coordinating."

Ahmed switched to the international emergency frequency, following standard protocols even though he expected no response from aircraft obviously committed to their attack mission. "Indian aircraft, this is Pakistan Air Force. You are in violation of Pakistani airspace. Turn back immediately or you will be fired upon."

No response, as expected.

He tried again, this time in Hindi to ensure there could be no misunderstanding: "Bharatiya vimaan, aap Pakistan ke hawaai kshetra mein hain. Turant vapas jaiye ya aap par hamla kiya jayega." ("Indian aircraft, you are in Pakistani airspace. Turn back immediately or you will be attacked.")

Still nothing. But Ahmed wasn't surprised by the lack of response. The Indians were clearly committed to their mission, and routine warnings weren't going to deter aircraft carrying out what appeared to be a carefully planned retaliation for the morning's terrorist attack.

Through his helmet's sophisticated heads-up display, Ahmed could see that the Indian formation had split into three two-aircraft groups, demonstrating the kind of tactical coordination that indicated thorough mission planning. Two aircraft were heading toward a target near Balakot, where intelligence reports suggested there was a facility used for training anti-India militants, while the other four were vectoring toward targets further north, including locations where Chinese technical assistance was reportedly being provided to enhance Pakistani capabilities.

What the Indian pilots didn't realize was that their electronic emissions—radar signals, communications, navigation systems, and electronic countermeasures—were being systematically monitored and analyzed by sophisticated Chinese-supplied electronic intelligence systems that had been integrated into Pakistan's air defense network. Pakistani operators were building a comprehensive, real-time picture of Indian aircraft capabilities, communications protocols, and tactical intentions that would inform not just this engagement, but future encounters between the two air forces.

"Thunder Leader, Control. The Indians have just struck their first target. Significant explosion observed at Grid Reference 341527. Electronic warfare assets report successful disruption of Indian tactical communications and some navigation systems. You are cleared to engage when ready."

Ahmed's finger moved to the weapons release button as he simultaneously activated electronic warfare systems that the Indian pilots would not be expecting and which his own training had only recently incorporated. Chinese-supplied electronic attack pods integrated with his F-16's systems were already beginning to create a complex electromagnetic environment that would interfere with Indian aircraft systems in ways the Rafale pilots had never experienced in training or previous operations.

"Thunder Flight, this is Leader. Engaging hostile aircraft. Electronic attack commencing. Fox Three!" The call indicated launch of an AIM-120 AMRAAM missile, the most sophisticated air-to-air weapon in Pakistan's inventory.

The radar-guided missile dropped away from Ahmed's F-16 and ignited its solid-fuel motor, streaking through the darkening sky toward the Indian formation at nearly four times the speed of sound. But simultaneously, the sophisticated electronic warfare systems that Chinese assistance had integrated into Pakistani air defenses were creating a complex electromagnetic environment that would challenge Indian pilots in ways they had never experienced during training exercises or previous conflicts.

Behind him, his wingman Flight Lieutenant Asad Malik was already launching his own missile at a second Indian aircraft while ground-based electronic warfare systems coordinated sophisticated jamming attacks designed to degrade Indian communications, radar systems, and navigation capabilities. The sky was suddenly full of missile contrails, radar warnings, and the controlled chaos of high-speed air-to-air combat—but also filled with invisible electronic attacks that were systematically degrading Indian capabilities in real-time.

"Control, Thunder Leader. Missiles away. Electronic warfare stations report successful target acquisition degradation on multiple hostile aircraft. Indian formation showing signs of significant navigation and communication difficulties. Request permission to press the attack."

"Thunder Leader, Control. Excellent work. Electronic warfare assessment indicates Indian formation coordination has been significantly disrupted. Multiple aircraft appear to be experiencing systems difficulties. Maintain your current station and prepare for follow-on engagements."

The Price of War

May 7, 2025 - 7:31 PM

Wing Commander Singh's Rafale

The first indication that something was seriously wrong came not from visual contact with enemy aircraft or standard missile warning systems, but from the sudden, systematic degradation of Singh's aircraft's electronic systems that began almost the moment his formation crossed into Pakistani airspace. His tactical datalink display flickered and disappeared entirely, his normally rock-solid radar began showing interference patterns he had never seen in training, and his radio communications became filled with static that made coordination with his wingmen increasingly difficult.

"Garuda Flight, we're being jammed heavily!" he called over the radio, fighting through the electronic interference while trying to maintain mission focus. "This is a much more sophisticated electronic warfare environment than intelligence briefings suggested. Pakistani capabilities appear significantly more advanced than assessed."

The carefully planned surgical strike was rapidly transforming into something far more complex and dangerous than any previous operation Singh had flown. His formation had successfully reached and destroyed their primary targets—the bomb damage assessment would later confirm that all three terrorist training facilities had been completely obliterated—but now they had to fight their way home through an electronic warfare environment unlike anything they had trained for or previously encountered.

"Missile launch detected! Break right! Break right!" The urgent warning tone in his headset was accompanied by his aircraft's defensive systems automatically dispensing chaff and flares while trying to cope with jamming that was affecting even basic defensive capabilities.

Singh yanked his Rafale into a violent defensive turn, pulling G-forces that pressed him deep into his ejection seat and tested both his physical conditioning and the aircraft's structural limits. Behind him, he could see the white smoke trail of a Pakistani missile streaking through the air where his aircraft had been only seconds before, but his defensive systems were struggling to function effectively in the intense electronic warfare environment that Pakistani forces had created.

"Garuda Flight, we're under attack from multiple directions!" he managed to call over the radio through the sophisticated jamming that was affecting virtually every electronic system on his aircraft. "Pakistani fighters inbound from the northeast and we have multiple missile launches! Electronic warfare is significantly degrading our systems across all spectrums!"

The engagement was taking place at supersonic speeds, with aircraft maneuvering violently through three-dimensional space while sophisticated electronic systems worked either to kill or save their pilots. But Singh's normally reliable radar was being systematically jammed by electronic warfare systems far more advanced than intelligence assessments had indicated, and his defensive systems were operating at reduced effectiveness due to the complex electromagnetic environment.

His Rafale's SPECTRA electronic warfare system, considered among the world's most advanced and a key reason for India's confidence in the aircraft's survivability, was being seriously challenged by Chinese-derived electronic attack systems that demonstrated capabilities approaching those of major powers rather than regional military forces. The electronic environment was more complex, more threatening, and more professionally executed than anything he had experienced during extensive training exercises against simulated advanced threats.

"Garuda Three is hit! Mayday! Mayday!" The panicked voice of Flight Lieutenant Gupta crackled over the radio through the jamming. Singh looked back through his cockpit canopy to see his wingman's aircraft trailing smoke and fire, the young pilot fighting desperately to maintain control while sophisticated electronic attacks continued to interfere with his damaged aircraft's systems.

"Mayday, mayday, this is Garuda Three. I'm losing hydraulics and engine power rapidly. Electronic systems are heavily degraded and I'm having difficulty maintaining controlled flight. Attempting emergency procedures but preparing to eject."

Singh watched helplessly as Gupta's aircraft began an uncontrolled spiral toward the mountainous terrain below. Every instinct told him to stay and help his wingman, to provide cover during the ejection and rescue, but Pakistani fighters were closing fast and his own aircraft was struggling with electronic interference that was affecting everything from basic navigation to weapons systems targeting.

The sophistication of the electronic warfare environment was genuinely shocking to Singh, who had been briefed on Pakistani capability improvements but had never imagined they could achieve this level of electronic attack coordination. Intelligence assessments had mentioned Chinese assistance and Pakistani upgrades, but this level of systematic electronic warfare capability suggested foreign technical support that went far beyond traditional arms sales into comprehensive capability development.

At the last possible second, Singh saw Gupta's ejection seat fire with a bright flash, throwing the young pilot clear of his doomed fighter. A parachute bloomed in the gathering darkness, carrying Flight Lieutenant Gupta down into Pakistani territory where he would become a prisoner of war in a conflict that was revealing fundamental shifts in military technology and regional strategic balance.

Singh was already turning for home, his remaining aircraft struggling to form up around him as they raced back toward the Line of Control through increasingly hostile airspace. Behind them, Pakistani fighters gave determined chase, their missiles lighting up the night sky while sophisticated electronic warfare systems continued to degrade Indian capabilities in ways that would require fundamental revision of tactical approaches.

The mission had achieved its primary tactical objectives—all three terrorist training facilities had been destroyed along with Chinese technical assistance infrastructure that intelligence had identified. But the strategic implications of the engagement were deeply troubling for Indian military planning. Pakistani electronic warfare capabilities had proven far more sophisticated than intelligence had indicated, suggesting that Chinese technology transfer had created a fundamental shift in the regional military balance that would require comprehensive strategic reassessment.

By the time Singh finally landed back at Srinagar Air Base, his aircraft's systems still showing the effects of electronic interference, he knew that the careful assumptions underlying Indian military planning would need to be completely revised. The technological balance of power that had favored Indian forces in previous conflicts had shifted more dramatically than anyone in New Delhi had realized, and Pakistan now possessed defensive capabilities that could challenge India's most advanced systems in ways that traditional superiority metrics had not anticipated.

The age of assured Indian electronic warfare superiority in South Asia was over, ended by Chinese technology transfer that had created new regional strategic realities. The implications of that fundamental shift would reverberate far beyond this single engagement, affecting everything from tactical planning to strategic doctrine to crisis management approaches throughout the region.

As Singh walked away from his aircraft and toward the debriefing that would reveal the full scope of the intelligence failure that had enabled Pakistani defensive success, he reflected on the uncomfortable reality that his state-of-the-art Rafale fighter had been systematically outmaneuvered by electronic warfare capabilities that supposedly didn't exist in the Pakistani inventory.

The world hears of the strike

May 9, 2025 - 9:00 PM

World media

BBC World Service Radio

"This is London. You're listening to the BBC World Service. I'm James Morrison with breaking news from South Asia."

"Indian military sources are confirming that they have conducted what they're calling 'surgical strikes' against terrorist targets inside Pakistan. The strikes, which took place at sunset local time, were in retaliation for this morning's terrorist attack that killed twenty-three Hindu pilgrims in Kashmir."

"Pakistani sources report that Indian aircraft violated their airspace and bombed what they describe as civilian areas. Pakistani forces engaged the Indian aircraft, claiming to have shot down at least one fighter jet."

"For analysis, I'm joined by Professor Sarah Ahmed from the School of Oriental and African Studies at the University of London. Professor Ahmed, how significant is this escalation?"

"James, this is extremely serious. We're seeing the same pattern that led to the 2019 Balakot crisis, but with both sides now possessing much more advanced military capabilities. The fact that there are already reports of aircraft being shot down suggests this could escalate much more rapidly than previous confrontations."

"What are the nuclear implications?"

"Both countries maintain what they call 'minimum deterrence' nuclear doctrines, meaning they keep their weapons as a last resort for existential threats. But Pakistan has been developing what they call 'tactical' nuclear weapons designed for battlefield use, which lowers the threshold for nuclear conflict."

"And international reaction?"

"The international community will be deeply concerned. Any conflict between nuclear powers threatens global stability. We're likely to see immediate diplomatic efforts to de-escalate, particularly from the United States, China, and other major powers."

"Professor Ahmed, thank you. We'll continue monitoring this developing story throughout

Social Media Explosion

May 9, 2025 - Various Times Twitter/X, Facebook, Instagram

@IndianAirForce (Verified) - "Indian Air Force carried out precision strikes on terror launch pads across LoC in response to Pahalgam attack #SurgicalStrike2025 #Justice" *147,000 retweets, 892,000 likes*

@rashtrapatibhvn (Verified) - President of India - "India stands united against terrorism. Our brave armed forces have delivered a befitting response to those who target innocent pilgrims. Jai Hind!" *203,000 retweets, 1.2M likes*

@OfficialDGISPR (Verified) - Pakistan Army - "Pakistan Air Force successfully intercepted Indian aircraft violating our airspace. One enemy aircraft shot down. Pilot captured. Pakistan reserves right to respond at time and place of our choosing." *89,000 retweets, 456,000 likes*

@ImranKhanPTI - "India's unprovoked aggression against Pakistan will not go unanswered. We are a peace-loving nation but will defend every inch of our territory! Pakistan Zindabad" *156,000 retweets, 678,000 likes*

@BBCBreaking (Verified) - "BREAKING: Pakistan confirms shooting down Indian fighter jet, pilot captured. India claims successful strikes on 'terror camps.' Both nuclear powers now in direct military confrontation." *67,000 retweets, 234,000 likes*

@CNN (Verified) - "URGENT: US officials concerned about escalation between India and Pakistan following air strikes and shoot-down. Both countries possess nuclear weapons." *45,000 retweets, 189,000 likes*

User posts flooding social media:

@RajeshMumbai47 - "My cousin died in Pahalgam attack. Thank you @IndianAirForce for showing these terrorists that India will not tolerate attacks on innocent Hindus. Jai Hind."

@PeaceLover_Delhi - "This is madness! One terrorist attack and now we're shooting at each other? Where does this end? Think of the families on both sides! #PeaceNotWar"

@ProudPakistani99 - "India thinks they can bomb Pakistan and face no consequences? Our pilots showed them that Pakistan's skies are defended! #DefendPakistan"

@KashmiriVoice - "Kashmir burns while politicians in Delhi and Islamabad play war games. When will the people of Kashmir get peace? #KashmirNeedspeace"

@GeneralArmchair - "Nuclear powers shooting at each other. Stock markets crashing. Oil prices spiking. Someone needs to stop this before it gets completely out of control. Where is @POTUS?"

@MotherOfTwo_UK - "Watching the news from India and Pakistan with growing horror. My heart goes out to the families of the pilgrims and the pilot. Please, someone stop this madness before more die."

Misinformation spreading rapidly:

FAKE: "BREAKING: Pakistan threatens nuclear strike if India continues attacks" (shared 45,000 times before fact-checkers flag)

FAKE: "Indian pilot admits mission was to bomb civilian targets" (shared 67,000 times)

FAKE: "US moving aircraft carrier to Arabian Sea to support India" (shared 23,000 times)

Operation Bunyan Ul Marsoos

May 10 2025 - 2:00 AM – 4:00 AM

Across the world

Pakistani Inter-Services Intelligence Headquarters, Islamabad

2:00 AM

Lieutenant General Asad Malik stood before a large wall-mounted map of the India-Pakistan border region, studying the detailed damage reports from the Indian air strikes with a complex mixture of professional satisfaction and strategic concern. Red pins marked the locations where Pakistani territory had been attacked, creating a visual record of Indian aggression, but green pins showed the successful engagements where Pakistani forces had demonstrated their dramatically enhanced capabilities against advanced Indian systems.

At 55, Malik had spent his entire professional career in Pakistan's intelligence services, rising through the ranks during the most turbulent and dangerous period in the country's history. He had witnessed the Soviet invasion of Afghanistan and Pakistan's role in supporting the mujahideen, the rise and fall of the Taliban, the American war on terror and its complex implications for Pakistani security, and countless crises with India that had brought the two nuclear powers to the brink of catastrophic conflict.

But this crisis felt fundamentally different from previous confrontations. The technological balance had shifted in ways that created entirely new strategic opportunities while simultaneously generating new risks that required careful management. The successful demonstration of Pakistani capabilities against Indian systems represented a validation of years of strategic planning and Chinese technical assistance, but it also created new pressures for escalation that could rapidly spiral beyond anyone's control.

"What do we know about the Indian pilot we captured?" asked General Khalil Bajwa, the Army Chief of Staff, who had arrived for an emergency briefing despite the late hour and the obvious exhaustion that marked all senior Pakistani officials during this crisis.

"We have Flight Lieutenant Rahul Gupta in secure custody," Malik reported, consulting his classified briefing folder. "He ejected over our territory and was captured by local security forces without incident. He's being held at a secure facility near Rawalpindi and is being treated according to Geneva Convention requirements. More importantly for our strategic assessment, our electronic warfare capabilities performed far better than the Indians expected, or our own most optimistic projections suggested."

"Describe the engagement results in detail."

"Significant tactical and strategic success across multiple domains," Malik replied, his professional satisfaction evident despite his attempts to maintain objective analysis. "Our J-10CE aircraft with integrated Chinese electronic warfare systems demonstrated clear superiority over Indian Rafales in the electronic domain. We successfully jammed their tactical communications, significantly degraded their radar performance, and achieved what appears to be the first-ever electronic warfare victory by Pakistani forces over advanced Western aircraft systems."

General Bajwa studied the tactical map with growing satisfaction, but also with the strategic caution that had characterized his leadership of Pakistani military forces. The red pins marking Indian strikes were unquestionably located inside Pakistani territory, representing clear violations of sovereignty that demanded response under both international law and domestic political pressure. But the green pins marking Pakistani successes represented something potentially more significant—proof that Pakistani forces could hold their own against India's most advanced systems.

"So, the Indians crossed our international border, bombed our sovereign territory, and we shot down one of their most expensive aircraft while demonstrating electronic warfare superiority that no one expected," Bajwa said slowly, absorbing the full implications. "This fundamentally changes the strategic calculation for any future conflict."

"Agreed completely," Malik replied, spreading additional intelligence assessments across the briefing table. "But we need to be strategically intelligent about our response. The Americans are already calling for restraint and will increase pressure if we appear to be escalating. The Chinese are watching very closely to assess how their technology performs in actual combat. If we escalate too far or too fast, we could find ourselves diplomatically isolated precisely when we need international support. But if we don't respond decisively to Indian aggression, we waste the strategic advantage our new capabilities have created."

Malik opened a secure intelligence file containing detailed assessments of Indian military positions along the Line of Control, satellite imagery of potential targets, and tactical plans that had been continuously updated based on evolving intelligence about Indian capabilities and likely responses. "I recommend Operation Bunyan Ul Marsoos—coordinated precision strikes against Indian military targets along the Line of Control, but with full utilization of our enhanced electronic warfare capabilities to demonstrate that last night's success wasn't a fluke. We need to show them that we can match their capabilities across the full spectrum of modern conflict."

The two men studied detailed reconnaissance photographs of Indian military installations positioned just across the disputed border. Artillery positions that had been harassing Pakistani civilians, radar stations that provided early warning for Indian air operations, supply depots that supported Indian military presence in Kashmir—all legitimate military targets that could be struck while demonstrating the full scope of Pakistani technological advancement.

"What about our nuclear posture?" Bajwa asked quietly, raising the question that hung over every Indo-Pakistani crisis like a shadow of potential civilization-ending catastrophe.

The question carried new weight and complexity in light of the night's demonstration of Pakistani conventional capabilities. Enhanced conventional capabilities created new strategic options for defending Pakistani territory without resorting to nuclear weapons, but they also created new risks if the Indians became desperate enough to escalate beyond conventional means to overcome Pakistani technological advantages.

"No changes to our nuclear alert status for now," Malik replied carefully, his years of strategic planning evident in his measured response. "But I recommend we prepare the Strategic Forces Command for potential escalation scenarios. The Indians may be tempted to escalate beyond conventional means if they realize their technological assumptions were fundamentally wrong. Our enhanced conventional capabilities provide improved deterrence, but we need nuclear deterrence as ultimate backup."

"How do we define 'too far' in the current strategic environment?"

"The same red lines that have always governed our nuclear doctrine," Malik replied, though both men understood that enhanced conventional capabilities might affect how those red lines were interpreted. "If they attack our major population centers or critical infrastructure. If they threaten to cut the country in half through ground operations across Punjab. If they attempt to occupy significant Pakistani territory or threaten the survival of the Pakistani state. These would represent existential threats that might require nuclear response regardless of our conventional capabilities."

General Bajwa nodded thoughtfully, understanding that enhanced conventional capabilities created both opportunities and responsibilities. "The Chinese will want a comprehensive assessment of how their technology performed in actual combat."

"Already prepared and ready for transmission," Malik replied, indicating a thick secure briefing folder marked with Chinese classification symbols. "Comprehensive technical assessment, detailed engagement timelines, electronic warfare effectiveness analysis, lessons learned, and recommendations for future capability enhancement. The Chinese investment in our defensive capabilities has been validated in combat against the most advanced Western systems. That success significantly strengthens our strategic relationship and provides leverage for additional technology transfer."

But Malik was also aware that success beyond expectations could be as destabilizing as failure. When tactical victories exceed strategic expectations, they often trigger desperate responses from adversaries who cannot accept defeat within existing strategic frameworks. Pakistani electronic warfare success had been so complete that it challenged Indian assumptions about technological superiority that formed the foundation of their strategic planning.

The technological balance that had defined Indo-Pakistani competition for decades had shifted more fundamentally than anyone had anticipated, creating new strategic realities that would require adaptation by all parties involved in South Asian security dynamics. The question now was whether that adaptation could occur through peaceful strategic adjustment or would require additional confrontation to establish new equilibrium between competing capabilities and strategic objectives.

The success of Chinese technology transfer to Pakistan had created a new model of strategic competition that could potentially be replicated in other regions where major powers competed through proxy relationships. If comprehensive technology assistance could enable smaller powers to challenge larger adversaries effectively, it would fundamentally alter global strategic competition and create new forms of interstate relationships that existing alliance frameworks might not adequately address.

The escalation that was about to unfold would test not just Pakistani and Indian capabilities, but the entire framework of crisis management and strategic competition in an era where technology transfer could rapidly alter regional balances and create strategic surprises that traditional intelligence assessment methods could not anticipate or prevent.

Al Jazeera English Live Report

May 10, 2025 - 4:00 AM IST

Anchor Farah Hassan: "Good afternoon, this is Al Jazeera English with continuing coverage of the escalating conflict between India and Pakistan. Artillery fire has been exchanged along the Line of Control for the past six hours, with both sides reporting casualties."

"I'm joined now by our correspondent Mehreen Shah, who is reporting from Islamabad. Mehreen, what's the latest on the Pakistani response?"

Correspondent Mehreen Shah: "Farah, the Pakistani military has confirmed what they're calling 'Operation Ghazi' - coordinated strikes against Indian military positions along the Line of Control. This appears to be a measured but significant escalation from yesterday's air strikes."

"The Pakistani Foreign Ministry has also summoned the Indian High Commissioner to lodge a formal protest over what they're calling 'unprovoked aggression against Pakistani territory.'"

Hassan: "Any word on the captured Indian pilot?"

Shah: "Pakistani officials say Flight Lieutenant Rahul Gupta is being treated according to the Geneva Conventions and is in good health. There are suggestions that he could be released as a goodwill gesture, but no firm commitment yet."

"What's significant, Farah, is that despite the military escalation, both governments are still using diplomatic language and avoiding the kind of rhetoric that could make de-escalation impossible."

Hassan: "And the international response?"

Shah: "Growing concern. The Chinese government has called for immediate de-escalation and offered to mediate. The EU has issued a statement calling for restraint. Most significantly, we're hearing that President Trump is personally engaging with both Prime Ministers to try to prevent further escalation."

"The key question now is whether either side has the political space to step back. Both governments are under enormous domestic pressure to appear strong, which makes de-escalation more difficult."

Hassan: "Mehreen Shah in Islamabad, thank you. When we return, we'll look at the global economic impact of this crisis..."

The Prisoner of War

May 10, 2025 - 8:00 AM

Detention Facility, Rawalpindi, Pakistan

Flight Lieutenant Rahul Gupta sat in a bare concrete cell, his familiar olive-green flight suit replaced with simple prison clothing that marked his transition from Indian Air Force pilot to prisoner of war in a conflict that seemed to be spiraling rapidly out of anyone's control. His ejection from the downed Rafale had been textbook perfect—a testament to French engineering and his own training—but landing in enemy territory remained every fighter pilot's nightmare scenario regardless of how professionally it was handled.

At 26 years old, Gupta was a graduate of the prestigious National Defence Academy who had dreamed of being a fighter pilot since childhood, inspired by stories of Indian Air Force heroism and motivated by a genuine desire to serve his country. His parents, middle-class professionals from Madhya Pradesh, had been enormously proud when he was selected to fly the Rafale, India's most advanced fighter aircraft and a symbol of the country's growing technological sophistication.

But what troubled Gupta most during his first night in Pakistani custody wasn't his uncertain future or even his separation from family—it was the sophisticated electronic warfare environment that had systematically degraded his aircraft's systems and ultimately contributed to his shoot-down. During the engagement, his Rafale's supposedly advanced defensive systems had been challenged by electronic attacks more sophisticated and coordinated than anything he had encountered during extensive training exercises.

The technological assumptions underlying Indian Air Force training and tactical doctrine appeared to have been fundamentally incorrect, raising disturbing questions about the intelligence assessments that guided Indian military planning and the strategic assumptions that shaped national security policy.

A Pakistani officer entered the cell carrying a folder and a steaming cup of tea, his approach professional and non-threatening. He was middle-aged with graying hair and the unmistakable bearing of a career military officer, his uniform indicating intelligence services rather than regular air force or army. His manner suggested extensive experience with prisoner handling and interrogation procedures.

"Good morning, Lieutenant. I am Colonel Mahmood of the Inter-Services Intelligence. I trust you are being treated appropriately according to Geneva Convention requirements?"

Gupta nodded, acknowledging that his treatment had indeed been correct and professional. The Geneva Conventions required humane treatment of prisoners of war, and so far the Pakistanis had scrupulously honored those international obligations. He had received immediate medical attention for minor ejection injuries, adequate food and water, basic hygiene facilities, and most importantly, no physical mistreatment or psychological pressure.

"Yes, sir. Though naturally I would prefer to be released and returned to my unit."

"That may certainly be possible in due course," Mahmood replied, settling into a simple metal chair and offering the tea with a gesture that seemed genuinely hospitable. "But first, I need to understand what happened yesterday evening. Your aircraft crossed into Pakistani airspace without authorization and participated in bombing attacks against what you claim were terrorist facilities but which we consider sovereign Pakistani territory."

"Those were not civilian facilities," Gupta replied firmly, his training in prisoner procedures guiding his response. "They were terrorist training camps used to plan and prepare attacks against innocent Indian civilians. The same terrorists who murdered twenty-three pilgrims yesterday morning."

Mahmood opened his folder, revealing photographs and documents that included detailed technical analysis of the electronic warfare engagement, aircraft performance data, and intelligence assessments that suggested Pakistani understanding of the encounter was far more comprehensive than Gupta had expected. "That is certainly your government's position. But let me ask you something as one professional military officer to another: were you surprised by our electronic warfare capabilities?"

The question caught Gupta off guard because it moved beyond traditional interrogation focused on intelligence extraction into professional discussion of military capabilities and tactical performance. Military interrogators typically sought specific information about unit capabilities, future operations, or technical specifications, not broad professional assessments.

"I... I follow orders and complete assigned missions. My specific mission was to destroy terrorist training facilities that threatened Indian security."

"Of course, and I respect your loyalty to your mission and your country," Mahmood replied patiently. "But as an experienced pilot flying one of the world's most advanced aircraft, you must have noticed that your sophisticated systems didn't perform exactly as you expected them to. Your radar was systematically jammed, your communications were seriously disrupted, your tactical datalinks failed completely. Did your extensive training and mission briefings prepare you for that level of electronic warfare sophistication?"

Gupta remained silent, but Mahmood's observations were uncomfortably accurate. The electronic environment during the engagement had been far more challenging and professionally executed than any training scenario or intelligence briefing had suggested Pakistani forces could create.

"Lieutenant, I'm not asking for classified military secrets or information that would compromise your oath as an officer," Mahmood continued, his tone remaining professional and respectful. "I'm simply asking whether your commanders and intelligence services understood what they were sending you and your colleagues into. Because based on the tactical intelligence briefings you undoubtedly received, I strongly suspect they didn't."

Mahmood showed Gupta a high-resolution photograph of his downed Rafale, the twisted wreckage a sobering reminder of how quickly advanced technology could be reduced to burning metal. "This aircraft represents the absolute pinnacle of French military aviation technology. It cost the Indian taxpayers over 200 million dollars per unit. Your extensive training probably emphasized its technological superiority over any aircraft or air defense system in this region. But yesterday, Pakistani pilots flying aircraft that cost one-fifth as much achieved electronic warfare dominance that brought down one of the world's most advanced fighters."

The implications of Mahmood's words were deeply troubling for anyone trained in Indian Air Force doctrine, which emphasized technological superiority as the foundation of tactical advantage. If Pakistani electronic warfare capabilities were indeed superior to Indian systems across significant operational scenarios, it suggested fundamental miscalculations in Indian strategic planning and defense procurement.

"What exactly do you want from me?" Gupta asked directly.

"Nothing that you cannot provide with complete honor as an officer and a gentleman," Mahmood replied sincerely. "But I want you to think carefully about something: your government sent you on a mission based on intelligence assessments that appear to have been fundamentally incorrect. They told you that Pakistani capabilities were inferior to Indian systems, but you experienced something very different during actual combat. Perhaps there are other things your government doesn't fully understand about this evolving conflict."

Through the small, barred window of his cell, Gupta could hear the distant sound of jet aircraft taking off, probably Pakistani fighters heading toward Indian positions for retaliatory strikes. The war was continuing and potentially escalating, and more pilots on both sides would soon face the same technological surprises that had resulted in his capture.

"My colleagues in Beijing are extremely interested in your aircraft's performance characteristics," Mahmood continued, making the Chinese connection explicit. "Your Rafale was equipped with the very latest French electronic warfare systems, including the highly advanced SPECTRA self-protection suite that European manufacturers claim can defeat any regional threat. The fact that our integrated systems could systematically defeat such advanced Western technology validates years of development, substantial investment, and comprehensive technical cooperation."

The direct mention of Beijing confirmed what Indian intelligence had suspected but apparently underestimated—comprehensive Chinese involvement in Pakistani capability enhancement that went far beyond traditional arms sales into systematic technology transfer and capability development.

"Lieutenant, you have become a symbol now," Mahmood observed thoughtfully. "An Indian pilot in Pakistani custody, but also a pilot whose extremely advanced aircraft was defeated by defensive systems that your intelligence services probably dismissed as technically inferior. How this situation is ultimately resolved could significantly influence whether this conflict expands into something much larger or contracts back toward diplomatic resolution."

Mahmood stood to leave, then paused at the cell door with what appeared to be genuine personal reflection. "I have a son about your age. He's studying engineering in Lahore with Chinese technical assistance, hoping to build systems that will improve people's lives rather than destroy them. Your parents probably have similar hopes—that their son will serve his country honorably and return home safely to build a better future. Perhaps both our countries would benefit from understanding how dramatically the technological balance has changed."

As Mahmood left the cell, Gupta stared out the small window at the gray morning sky, wondering if his capture might somehow become a catalyst for preventing an even greater catastrophe. But he was also wondering whether Indian military planning was based on technological assumptions that no longer reflected the strategic reality of South Asian competition.

The conversation with Colonel Mahmood had revealed something that Gupta found deeply disturbing: Pakistani confidence wasn't based on bravado or propaganda, but on genuine technological capabilities that had been tested in combat and found effective against the most advanced systems in the Indian inventory. This wasn't the desperate bluster of an inferior force trying to compensate for technological disadvantages—this was the quiet confidence of professionals who knew exactly what their systems could do because they had just proven it in actual combat.

Financial Times - Morning Edition

May 10, 2025

MARKETS PLUNGE AS INDIA-PAKISTAN CRISIS DEEPENS

Nuclear fears drive global sell-off as military escalation continues

Global stock markets suffered their worst day in over a year yesterday as the military confrontation between India and Pakistan entered its second day with no signs of de-escalation.

The FTSE 100 closed down 4.2%, while the Dow Jones fell 3.8% in early trading before US markets closed for emergency consultation with the Federal Reserve. Asian markets fared worse, with the Nikkei dropping 6.1% and Hong Kong's Hang Seng falling 5.7%.

"This is exactly the kind of geopolitical risk that markets can't price," said Jennifer Morgan, chief strategist at Goldman Sachs International. "When you have two nuclear powers in direct military confrontation, traditional risk models break down."

Oil prices spiked 12% on fears that conflict could disrupt shipping through the Arabian Sea, while gold surged to its highest level since 2020 as investors fled to safe-haven assets.

The Indian rupee and Pakistani rupee both fell to multi-year lows against the dollar, while bond yields in both countries rose sharply as investors demanded higher premiums for holding the debt of nations at war.

"The immediate economic impact is already significant," noted Dr. Rajesh Chadha of the National Institute of Public Finance and Policy in New Delhi. "But if this escalates to prolonged conflict, we're looking at massive disruption to one of the world's most important economic regions."

The crisis has also affected global supply chains, with several major technology companies reporting potential disruptions to manufacturing operations in both countries. India and Pakistan together account for nearly 20% of global software development and a significant portion of textile manufacturing.

Central banks around the world have indicated they are prepared to intervene to maintain market stability, with the Federal Reserve, European Central Bank, and Bank of Japan all issuing statements emphasizing their readiness to provide liquidity if needed.

"This reminds me of the Cuban Missile Crisis in terms of market psychology," said veteran trader Michael Harrison. "When the survival of civilization is potentially at stake, normal investment calculations become meaningless."

Counter-Strike

1

2 May, 2025 - 07:30 PM

Indian Artillery Position, Kashmir

Major Shailesh Kumar heard the incoming Pakistani artillery shells long before the radio warning reached her mountainous position, the distinctive whistle-shriek of 155mm rounds cutting through the thin mountain air a sound that no combat veteran ever forgot once they'd experienced it under fire. But what followed the initial warning was unlike any artillery attack she had experienced during her twelve years of distinguished service in some of India's most challenging operational environments.

"Incoming fire! Take cover immediately!" he shouted, diving for the nearest reinforced bunker as explosions began erupting around her carefully positioned artillery battery with unprecedented precision that suggested Pakistani forces were using advanced targeting technology far beyond what intelligence assessments had indicated they possessed.

The Pakistani retaliation had begun at dawn with carefully coordinated strikes against Indian positions all along the Line of Control, but the sophistication of the attacks—their precision, timing, and integration with electronic warfare—suggested capabilities that intelligence assessments had fundamentally underestimated. Artillery barrages were hitting with GPS-level precision accuracy, electronic warfare systems were systematically jamming

Indian communications across broad frequency ranges, and what appeared to be coordinated cyber-attacks were disrupting command and control systems throughout the Indian operational area.

Major Shailesh, at 32, was a decorated officer who had commanded his six-gun artillery battery through three years of border tensions, counter-insurgency operations, and the constant low-level conflict that characterized the Line of Control. He had trained extensively for conventional artillery duels and integrated fire support operations, but the Pakistani response demonstrated a level of electronic warfare integration, precision targeting, and coordinated attack that approached the capabilities of major powers rather than regional military forces.

As the initial bombardment lifted—a temporary pause that experienced officers knew often preceded even heavier attacks—Shailesh emerged from his bunker to assess the damage and coordinate his unit's response. Two of his six 155mm howitzers had been destroyed by direct hits that could only have resulted from precision targeting, their crews lying motionless beside the twisted metal that had been some of India's most modern artillery pieces. Three additional soldiers were wounded and calling for medics, clutching shrapnel wounds while trying to maintain their positions.

But perhaps more concerning than the physical damage was the systematic failure of his communication systems. Radio equipment that had functioned perfectly that morning was now producing only static and interference, field telephones were dead, and even basic GPS navigation systems were showing error messages that suggested comprehensive electronic warfare rather than simple equipment failure.

"Major!" His radio operator came running across the rocky terrain with an urgent message that had been delivered by motorcycle courier since all radio communications remained completely jammed. "Fire mission from brigade headquarters. Pakistani armored column observed moving toward assault positions near the Line of Control. We're ordered to engage immediately with maximum available firepower, but all communications are being severely disrupted by sophisticated electronic warfare."

Shailesh studied the target coordinates on her tactical map while trying to understand how Pakistani forces had achieved such comprehensive electronic superiority over a battlefield where Indian forces had historically maintained technological advantages. The target was a Pakistani tank unit that appeared to be preparing for a ground assault across the disputed border, but her ability to coordinate effective fire support was being systematically degraded by electronic attacks that approached the sophistication of major power military capabilities.

"Load high explosive shells immediately," he ordered her remaining gun crews, who were working with the disciplined efficiency that had made Indian artillery effective despite technological disadvantages. "Range 8,400 meters, azimuth 047 degrees. Prepare for battery fire on my command but be aware that Pakistani electronic warfare is seriously affecting our fire control systems. We'll have to use manual procedures and backup targeting methods."

The shift to manual fire control procedures represented a significant tactical disadvantage that reduced both accuracy and response time, but it was absolutely necessary due to the sophisticated electronic warfare environment that Pakistani forces had created across the entire operational area. Intelligence assessments had mentioned Pakistani capability improvements but had not prepared Indian forces for this level of systematic electronic attack coordination.

"Major," his communications sergeant reported after attempting to contact higher headquarters through multiple backup systems, "we're receiving sophisticated interference across all available frequency bands. This isn't simple jamming or accidental interference, it's professional electronic attack that suggests advanced technology and extensive operator training rather than improvised capability."

In the distance, Pakistani guns were already adjusting their fire toward her position with precision that suggested advanced target acquisition capabilities and fire control systems that were apparently immune to the electronic warfare affecting Indian systems. The technological balance in South Asia had shifted more dramatically than anyone in New Delhi had anticipated, creating new tactical realities that would require fundamental adaptation in operational planning and strategic thinking.

"Major! Enemy aircraft inbound from the northwest!" his air defense observer called out urgently. "And our air defense radar systems are reporting significant electronic interference that's affecting target acquisition!"

The electronic warfare revolution was demonstrating how smaller powers could achieve tactical advantages over larger adversaries through superior integration and external technical assistance rather than indigenous development or resource advantages. If this model could be replicated elsewhere, it would fundamentally alter global strategic competition and create new forms of interstate relationships that existing alliance frameworks might not adequately address.

The Nuclear Shadow

May 13, 2025 - 1:00 AM

Strategic Forces Command, Islamabad

General Tariq Baig stood before the massive electronic status board displaying Pakistan's nuclear arsenal while contemplating how the previous day's dramatic technological demonstrations had fundamentally altered strategic calculations that had governed South Asian stability for decades. As commander of the Strategic Forces Command, he bore ultimate responsibility for the country's nuclear weapons, the absolute guarantors of national survival, but also the instruments of potentially unthinkable destruction that could end human civilization in South Asia.

At 58, General Baig had devoted his entire professional career to ensuring that Pakistan's nuclear weapons would never be used in anger, while simultaneously ensuring they remained credible enough to deter any existential threat to the Pakistani state. It was a profound responsibility that had shaped every aspect of his military service and strategic thinking. But the dramatic enhancement of Pakistani conventional capabilities through Chinese assistance had created entirely new strategic options and entirely new risks that traditional nuclear doctrine had not anticipated.

"Sir," his military aide announced with the crisp professionalism that characterized the Strategic Forces Command, "Prime Minister Shah has arrived for his scheduled briefing on nuclear posture and strategic implications."

Prime Minister Hamza Shah entered the underground command center looking visibly older than his 62 years, but also with an unmistakable hint of satisfaction at the tactical successes Pakistani forces had achieved over the past day and a half. The immense weight of leading a nuclear nation during a major crisis was clearly visible in the lines around his eyes and the careful way he moved, but Pakistani technological performance had provided new confidence in the country's ability to defend itself through conventional means.

"General, what is our current nuclear readiness posture?"

"Normal peacetime readiness level, sir. All systems remain functional and secure with no changes to standard operating procedures. We have deliberately made no alterations to our alert status despite the remarkable conventional success of our armed forces, and we're maintaining complete strategic stability."

"And Indian nuclear posture?"

"Our intelligence assessment suggests they also remain at normal readiness levels, but there are increasing signs of concern about our conventional capabilities that may be affecting their strategic calculations. Neither side wants to be the first to escalate to nuclear signaling, but the comprehensive demonstration of our technological advancement may be forcing Indian strategic planners to reconsider fundamental assumptions."

Shah studied the large electronic map showing the real-time locations of Indian and Pakistani forces engaged in conventional combat across the disputed border region. Red and blue symbols marked ongoing artillery exchanges, air patrol patterns, and ground positions where soldiers were actively shooting at each other across a border that had divided families and communities for over seven decades. But the technological balance displayed on the sophisticated monitoring systems was fundamentally different from any previous conflict in the region.

"Our conventional performance has dramatically exceeded all expectations," Shah observed with obvious satisfaction. "Chinese assistance has provided capabilities that fundamentally change the strategic calculation for any extended conflict."

"Absolutely correct, sir. Our electronic warfare success against Indian advanced systems, the precision of our artillery fire, the effectiveness of our integrated air defense network—all demonstrate capabilities that approach those of major powers rather than regional forces. This success significantly strengthens our conventional deterrence while reducing our dependence on nuclear threats to maintain strategic stability."

The secure briefing room fell silent as both men contemplated the complex implications of enhanced conventional capabilities for nuclear strategy and regional stability. Enhanced conventional capabilities could theoretically reduce nuclear risks by providing credible non-nuclear deterrence against a wide range of threats, but they could also increase risks by encouraging more aggressive policies or by prompting adversaries to escalate to nuclear levels to overcome conventional disadvantages.

"General, I want you to prepare—but not yet implement—a limited elevation of our nuclear readiness status. Not because we have any intention of using nuclear weapons, but because the Indians may be tempted to escalate beyond conventional means if they realize their fundamental technological assumptions were incorrect."

Baig nodded, understanding the strategic logic while recognizing the risks. "What specific red lines should guide our nuclear posture decisions?"

Shah considered the question with the care it deserved, understanding that enhanced conventional capabilities meant that nuclear thresholds could potentially be raised, but they also created new vulnerabilities if adversaries sought to negate conventional advantages through nuclear threats or limited nuclear use.

"The traditional red lines remain in effect," Shah replied thoughtfully. "If they attack our major population centers or critical civilian infrastructure. If they threaten Islamabad, Karachi, or other major cities. If they attempt to cut the country in half through ground operations across Punjab province. But I'm adding a new consideration: if they threaten our technological infrastructure—the facilities where Chinese assistance is provided, the systems that enable our conventional effectiveness, the strategic relationships that provide our capability advantages."

The addition of technology protection to nuclear response thresholds represented a significant innovation in Pakistani strategic thinking, reflecting how important Chinese-assisted capabilities had become to national security and how their protection might warrant ultimate escalation to preserve Pakistan's ability to defend itself conventionally.

"Understood completely, sir. I'll prepare the enhanced readiness protocols immediately but will await your direct personal authorization before any implementation."

"Also," Shah added, recognizing the broader strategic implications, "coordinate closely with our Chinese partners. They have made a substantial investment in the success of their military technology, and they need to understand how technological success affects regional strategic stability and their own interests."

"Should we inform them of potential nuclear posture changes?"

"Inform them of our strategic thinking but emphasize that enhanced conventional capabilities are designed to reduce rather than increase nuclear risks. But also include that we now hold any major reduction in water in the Sutlej as an existential threat. Leave it at that."

As Shah left the command center to return to other crisis management responsibilities, Baig remained alone with the electronic displays showing Pakistan's nuclear capabilities and contemplated the fundamental paradox that enhanced conventional capabilities had created.

The nuclear weapons that were supposed to provide ultimate security for both countries could become the instruments of mutual destruction if conventional setbacks triggered escalation spirals that neither side could control. The technological balance that Chinese assistance had created was fundamentally altering strategic calculations in ways that traditional nuclear doctrine might not adequately address.

The Chinese keep a watch

May 13, 2025 – 3:00 AM

Central Military Commission Headquarters, Beijing

General Liu Wei stood before a wall of high-resolution displays showing real-time satellite feeds of the South Asian conflict while senior Chinese military and political leadership absorbed the implications of their technology's combat performance. At 61, Liu commanded the People's Liberation Army's Equipment Development Department, responsible for the comprehensive technology transfer programs that had just demonstrated their effectiveness in the most dramatic possible way.

"Comrades," he began, addressing the emergency session of the Central Military Commission's Strategy Committee, "what we have witnessed in the past seventy-two hours represents validation of our strategic approach to technology proliferation and regional balance management that exceeds our most optimistic projections."

President Xi Jinping, participating via secure video link from a state visit to Africa, leaned forward with obvious interest. "General Liu, provide your comprehensive assessment of combat performance and strategic implications."

"Mr. President, our electronic warfare systems demonstrated clear superiority over French Rafale aircraft equipped with the most advanced Western defensive systems. Pakistani forces achieved systematic degradation of Indian communications, radar, and navigation systems across multiple engagement scenarios. Most significantly, they shot down an aircraft costing over 200 million dollars using systems we provided at a fraction of that cost."

Foreign Minister Wang Yi interjected with the diplomatic concerns that always shadowed military success. "General, while the technological validation is impressive, we must consider broader implications for our strategic relationships with both India and the international community. Indian government and military leadership have clearly been surprised by Pakistani capabilities, which could affect their future cooperation with Chinese economic initiatives."

Defense Minister Wei Fenghe spread detailed technical analysis across the conference table. "The electronic warfare integration performed beyond specifications. Pakistani operators demonstrated proficiency levels indicating their training programs were more effective than we projected. Most importantly, the coordination between multiple systems—radar, jamming, missile guidance, tactical communications—approached the seamless integration we expect from our own forces."

Liu nodded, reviewing comprehensive battle damage assessments that had been continuously updated throughout the crisis. "The strategic implications extend far beyond South Asia. We have demonstrated that comprehensive technology transfer can enable smaller powers to achieve tactical advantages over conventionally superior adversaries. This model can be replicated in multiple regions where we seek to alter balance dynamics without direct Chinese military involvement."

The statement reflected the broader strategic logic underlying Chinese technology proliferation—creating regional balances that served Chinese interests while maintaining plausible deniability about direct involvement in regional conflicts.

President Xi's voice carried the weight of someone contemplating global strategic implications. "General Liu, describe the replication potential. Where else might this approach prove effective?"

"Multiple regions offer similar opportunities, Mr. President. Southeast Asian partners facing conventional pressure from alliance structures. Middle Eastern partners seeking credible deterrence against technologically superior adversaries. African partners requiring defense against intervention capabilities. The Pakistani model demonstrates how rapidly regional balances can be altered through systematic capability enhancement."

But it was the unexpected voice of Vice Foreign Minister Le Yucheng that introduced the cautionary perspective that would ultimately shape Chinese policy. "Comrades, we must also consider escalation risks that technological success creates. Pakistani capabilities exceeded Indian intelligence assessments so dramatically that Indian political leadership may face pressure to escalate rather than accept conventional defeat. Enhanced capabilities can destabilize as well as stabilize if they create desperate responses from adversaries who cannot accept new strategic realities."

The room fell silent as participants absorbed the implications. Chinese technology transfer had been designed to enhance deterrence and regional stability, but dramatic success could trigger desperate responses that challenged crisis management frameworks.

"Vice Minister Le raises crucial considerations," Xi acknowledged. "General Liu, what are your recommendations for managing these escalation risks while maintaining the strategic advantages our technology transfer has created?"

Liu consulted his classified assessments while considering how to balance technological success with strategic stability. "Mr. President, I recommend we continue enhancing Pakistani capabilities to ensure sustainable deterrence, but we should also engage diplomatically to prevent Indian desperation from triggering nuclear escalation. Additionally, we should prepare contingency plans for scenarios where our technology transfer relationships create obligations for Chinese involvement that we must carefully manage."

"Explain the obligation scenarios in detail."

"Sir, if Pakistani forces become dependent on Chinese technology for their defensive effectiveness, attacks on that technology infrastructure could be interpreted as attacks on Chinese strategic interests. We may face pressure to defend not just Pakistani territory, but the technological systems that enable Pakistani defense capabilities."

The strategic complexity was staggering. Chinese investment in Pakistani capabilities created new forms of strategic interdependence that could draw China into conflicts it preferred to avoid while simultaneously serving Chinese strategic interests through proxy enhancement.

Defense Minister Wei added crucial operational considerations. "Our technical advisors embedded with Pakistani forces report extremely positive cooperation and genuine partnership development. The relationship has evolved beyond simple arms sales into comprehensive strategic cooperation that serves both sides' interests effectively."

"But," Vice Foreign Minister Le continued his cautionary analysis, "American diplomatic intervention has prevented escalation to levels that could have tested our obligations more severely. If the crisis had continued, we might have faced choices between abandoning Pakistani partners or accepting direct involvement in South Asian nuclear crisis."

President Xi synthesized the complex factors with the strategic clarity that had characterized his leadership. "Comrades, we will continue enhancing capabilities for partners facing conventional pressure, but we will simultaneously develop diplomatic mechanisms for managing escalation risks that technological success creates. The Pakistani model validates our approach while demonstrating the need for sophisticated crisis management that accounts for how rapidly technology transfer can alter regional dynamics."

The meeting concluded with directives for expanding the Pakistani model globally while developing safeguards against escalation risks that technological success could create. Chinese technology transfer had proven effective beyond expectations, but it had also revealed new challenges for managing strategic competition in an era where capability enhancement could rapidly alter regional balances and create new forms of strategic interdependence that traditional frameworks could not adequately address.

As participants filed out to implement policies that would reshape global strategic competition, General Liu remained behind, studying satellite feeds of Pakistani and Indian forces that were finally beginning to disengage under American diplomatic pressure.

The technological revolution that Chinese assistance had enabled was spreading globally, creating new paradigms for strategic competition that would require continuous adaptation by all major powers. The question was no longer whether technology transfer could rapidly alter regional balances—Pakistani success had proven that conclusively. The question was whether the international community could develop frameworks for managing the strategic implications responsibly before technological advantages triggered conflicts that could threaten human civilization itself.

The long game of strategic competition in the technology transfer era had only just begun, with implications that would reverberate globally for decades to come.

The First Call comes

May 13, 2025 - 4:00 AM

Prime Minister's Residence, New Delhi

The secure red phone jolted Rajesh Patel awake at precisely 1:00 AM. The caller ID showed the White House, but this conversation would address more than traditional crisis management—it would confront the complete collapse of India's international position.

"Prime Minister Patel? This is President Trump calling from Air Force One. I hope I'm not waking you up, though I guess at this hour I probably am. We need to talk immediately about what's happening between you and Pakistan, and frankly, some of the things our intelligence people are telling me about capabilities that nobody seems to have expected."

Patel sat up in bed, instantly alert despite his exhaustion and the late hour. A direct call from the American President at this time of night meant that Washington was viewing the crisis as an imminent threat to global stability, possibly with implications that extended far beyond South Asian regional security concerns.

"Mr. President, thank you for calling. I assume you're fully aware of the current situation and the technological surprises this conflict has revealed."

"Very aware, and frankly, I'm deeply concerned about several things our intelligence services are telling me about Pakistani capabilities that apparently exceeded everyone's expectations, including your own. This confrontation between India and Pakistan is escalating rapidly, and I think we need to have an honest conversation, leader to leader, about what's really happening and how we can dial this back before people start getting killed by the thousands."

Patel walked to the window of his bedroom, looking out at the lights of New Delhi spread before him in the pre-dawn darkness. Even at this hour, the capital city showed clear signs of the ongoing crisis—military convoys moving through major streets, government buildings illuminated with emergency meetings, and crowds of people gathered around news broadcasts despite the late hour, all reflecting a nation grappling with strategic realities that had shifted more rapidly than anyone had anticipated.

"Mr. President, with all due respect, people are already being killed in significant numbers. Twenty-three innocent pilgrims died in a sophisticated terrorist attack that originated from Pakistani territory with what appears to be Chinese technical assistance. We cannot simply ignore that aggression."

"I completely understand your anger and your need for justice, believe me. When people attack innocent Americans, my first instinct is always to hit back hard and decisively. But you've clearly made your point with those precision air strikes yesterday. And frankly, the Pakistanis seem to have made their own point with defensive capabilities that surprised a lot of very smart people in Washington who thought they understood the regional balance."

Trump's explicit reference to Pakistani capabilities suggested that American intelligence had been similarly surprised by the technological sophistication demonstrated during the conflict, indicating that the strategic implications extended beyond bilateral Indo-Pakistani relations to broader international strategic planning.

"What specifically are you suggesting, Mr. President?"

"I'm suggesting that maybe it's time for both sides to step back from further escalation and conduct a comprehensive reassessment of what we're all dealing with here. Our intelligence people are telling me that Pakistani electronic warfare capabilities not only matched but apparently exceeded your most advanced systems during yesterday's engagement. That changes the strategic picture significantly and requires new thinking about regional stability."

The acknowledgment confirmed what Indian military commanders had been reluctant to admit publicly—that Pakistani technological capabilities had fundamentally altered regional military balance in ways that strategic planning and intelligence assessments had not anticipated, requiring comprehensive revision of assumptions that had guided policy for decades.

"The Pakistani government continues to harbor and support terrorists, Mr. President. Until that fundamental problem is addressed, these attacks will continue and escalate. Our people deserve effective protection from increasingly sophisticated threats."

"Maybe you're right about Pakistani support for terrorism, but turning Kashmir into a major battlefield isn't going to eliminate terrorism, Prime Minister. And if the Pakistanis really do have the kind of advanced defensive capabilities our people think they demonstrated, this could escalate in ways that nobody wants and that could destabilize the entire region."

Trump's concerns reflected broader strategic implications of Pakistani technological advancement that created new variables in crisis management. Enhanced capabilities could increase Pakistani confidence in managing escalation, but they could also prompt Indian escalation to overcome conventional disadvantages or lead to miscalculations based on outdated assumptions about relative capabilities.

Patel remained quiet for a long moment, absorbing the implications while watching the vigil continuing in the streets below his window. Through the bulletproof glass, he could see protesters still gathered despite the late hour, holding candles and photographs of the Pahalgam victims while demanding justice for their deaths. But he was also thinking about the electronic warfare reports, the precision of Pakistani artillery, and the broader implications of Chinese technology transfer that appeared far more comprehensive than intelligence had assessed.

"The Pakistani Prime Minister would need to make significant concrete concessions," Patel said finally, outlining the minimum requirements for any negotiated settlement. "Immediate return of our captured pilot, comprehensive crackdown on terrorist groups operating from their territory, substantial compensation to the victims' families, credible guarantees that such attacks will not happen again, and most importantly, complete transparency about Chinese assistance and technology transfer that's created these new regional capabilities."

"What if I could personally arrange and guarantee all of that? What if I put my own credibility and the full weight of American influence behind ensuring that Pakistan meets every one of those conditions, plus provides detailed information about technology transfer relationships that affect regional stability, in exchange for an immediate ceasefire and comprehensive negotiations?"

"You would be willing to make such commitments?"

"Prime Minister, I've got two nuclear powers actively shooting at each other with military capabilities that seem to be evolving faster than anybody's strategic planning can keep up with. Yeah, I'd make those commitments and more to prevent World War Three, especially when it's being triggered by technology transfers that nobody fully understood until they were tested in actual combat."

The conversation continued for another thirty minutes, with Trump pressing for specific commitments while acknowledging the technological realities that had fundamentally altered strategic calculations throughout the region. When the call finally ended, Patel stood at his window for a long time, watching the ongoing vigil in the streets below while contemplating the fundamental revision of strategic assumptions that the crisis had forced upon all parties.

The families of the victims deserved justice for their murdered loved ones. But they also deserved to live in a world where such conflicts didn't escalate into nuclear catastrophes that could kill millions of innocent people. Most importantly, they deserved honest strategic assessments of the technological realities that would shape future conflicts and security planning throughout the region.

The question now was whether Pakistan would be willing to make the substantial concessions necessary for sustainable peace, and whether both sides could successfully adapt to a strategic environment where Chinese technology transfer had fundamentally altered the regional balance of power in ways that traditional strategic planning had not anticipated.

But even as Patel considered the American proposal, he was acutely aware that accepting any agreement that appeared to reward Pakistani technological success might encourage further Chinese technology transfer to other regional actors, potentially destabilizing strategic balance throughout Asia and requiring fundamental revision of Indian strategic planning across multiple theaters.

The world is alarmed

May 13, 2025

All over the world

United Nations Security Council, New York

10:00 AM

UN Secretary-General António Guterres called an emergency session of the Security Council as reports of nuclear-related activities in both India and Pakistan reached international intelligence agencies. The great hall of the UN building had seen many crises, but rarely one with such potential for global catastrophe.

"Colleagues," Guterres began, his Portuguese accent heavy with emotion, "we are facing a situation that demands immediate action from the international community. Two nuclear powers are engaged in direct military confrontation with signs of potential escalation toward weapons of mass destruction."

The American ambassador, Linda Thompson, spoke first: "The United States calls for immediate cessation of hostilities and return to diplomatic dialogue. We are prepared to use all diplomatic resources to facilitate de-escalation."

Chinese Ambassador Wu Haitao was equally direct: "China strongly condemns any escalation toward nuclear weapons and calls for both parties to step back from the brink. The use of nuclear weapons would be catastrophic for all humanity."

British Ambassador James Crawford: "The United Kingdom echoes the call for immediate de-escalation. We are prepared to join international mediation efforts to prevent this crisis from expanding further."

Russian Ambassador Sergey Petrov was more circumspect: "Russia calls for restraint from all parties. However, we must also recognize that nations have the right to defend themselves against terrorist attacks."

The Pakistani ambassador, Maleeha Lodhi, defended her country's position: "Pakistan has acted solely in self-defense against unprovoked Indian aggression. We call on the international community to condemn India's violation of Pakistani sovereignty."

Indian Ambassador T.S. Tirumurti responded: "India's actions were a measured response to terrorism sponsored from Pakistani territory. We seek only to protect our citizens from future attacks."

Maleeha Lodhi responded: "Even if it be agreed that it was a Pakistan sponsored attack, you should have provided some specifics and asked us to take action. It is our country. Moreover, we don't see any action pinpointing blame on the security and intelligence officials, tasked to protect your citizens. While that is entirely your internal matter, it becomes relevant when you decide to take unilateral action on that issue against a sovereign country."

As the debate continued, aides brought urgent messages to various ambassadors. The crisis was developing faster than the diplomatic machinery could respond.

Secretary-General Guterres concluded the session with an unprecedented statement: "I am personally appealing to the leaders of both nations to contact me immediately. The United Nations stands ready to provide any assistance necessary to prevent nuclear conflict. The survival of human civilization may depend on the decisions made in the next few hours."

A Secure Facility, Virginia
May 13, 2025 - 1:00 PM

CIA Director Sarah Chen sat in a windowless room deep beneath the agency's Langley headquarters, participating in a secure video conference with intelligence chiefs from India and Pakistan. These back-channel communications had been established years earlier as a way for the three nuclear powers to share critical information during crises without the political complications of formal diplomacy.

"Gentlemen," Chen began, addressing the encrypted video feeds showing her counterparts, "my government is extremely concerned about the nuclear signaling we're observing from both sides. Can you help us understand what we're seeing?"

General Malik from Pakistani ISI spoke first: "Director Chen, Pakistan has made no changes to our nuclear posture. Any increased activity you're observing is purely defensive in nature, responding to similar activities we're detecting from Indian facilities."

The Indian intelligence chief, K.V. Raman, responded immediately: "That is precisely our position as well. India has made no aggressive nuclear preparations, but we cannot ignore signs that Pakistan may be elevating their readiness status."

Chen suppressed a sigh. This was exactly the kind of circular misperception that could lead to catastrophe. "So each side is taking defensive measures in response to defensive measures from the other side?"

"Correct," both men said simultaneously.

"And neither side has any intention of actually using nuclear weapons?"

"Absolutely not," Malik replied. "Pakistan's nuclear doctrine is purely defensive."

"India has a clear no-first-use policy," Raman added. "We would never initiate nuclear conflict."

"Then help me understand something," Chen said. "If neither side wants nuclear escalation, why don't you just call each other directly and confirm that you're both taking purely defensive measures?"

The video conference fell silent. Chen realized she had identified the core of the problem: even the intelligence chiefs of two countries that had been neighbors for decades couldn't trust each other enough to have a simple conversation about preventing nuclear war.

"Perhaps," she suggested carefully, "the United States could serve as an intermediary to verify the defensive nature of both sides' nuclear activities?"

It was a proposal that would require unprecedented cooperation and trust. But as Chen looked at the faces on her screens, she realized it might be the only way to prevent a catastrophic misunderstanding.

The Crisis Deepens

May 14, 2025

Multiple Locations

3: 05 AM Pakistan

General Baig was reviewing overnight intelligence when his aide burst in with urgent reports. "Sir, significant Indian military movements toward the Line of Control. Multiple armored columns, additional artillery batteries, increased air activity. Intelligence suggests possible preparation for major ground offensive."

Baig studied intelligence summaries with growing alarm. If accurate, India might be preparing for ground assault that could threaten Pakistan's survival and trigger nuclear thresholds discussed with the Prime Minister.

"Confidence level?"

"High, sir. Multiple sources, including signal intercepts and satellite imagery."

What Baig didn't know was that Indian movements were defensive—repositioning forces to counter perceived Pakistani offensive preparations that were themselves defensive responses to Indian defensive measures.

8:40 AM New Delhi

In New Delhi, political pressure was mounting exponentially as leaked recordings continued dominating headlines:

Times of India: "Officials knew attack was coming, chose paperwork over people"

Hindustan Times: "How bureaucracy killed 23 pilgrims"

Indian Express: "Government cover-up after preventable deaths"

Opposition leader Rahul Gandhi was demanding Prime Minister Patel's resignation: "If the government had seventy-two hours' warning and chose bureaucratic procedures over citizen safety, they have blood on their hands."

Victim families were filing criminal cases against intelligence officials while demanding to know why their loved ones died from preventable institutional failures.

The domestic pressure was creating desperate incentives for escalation to deflect from accountability issues—exactly the dynamic that could trigger nuclear conflict.

Global intelligence services were detecting the nuclear preparation indicators and reaching alarming conclusions about escalation risks.

10:00 AM Indian Air Force Command, New Delhi

Air Marshal Rajendra Singh studied the intelligence reports with growing concern. Pakistani forces had moved additional aircraft to forward bases, artillery units were being reinforced along the Line of Control, and most worrying of all, there were signs of increased activity at Pakistani nuclear facilities.

As one of India's most senior military commanders, Singh had spent his career preparing for exactly this scenario – a major conventional conflict with Pakistan that could potentially escalate to nuclear exchange. But the theoretical had now become terrifyingly real.

"Sir," his intelligence officer reported, "we're seeing unusual movement patterns at their Strategic Forces Command headquarters. Increased communications traffic, additional security measures, and what appears to be a change in alert status for some strategic systems."

The Air Marshal felt a chill that had nothing to do with the air conditioning. These were exactly the kinds of indicators that intelligence analysts had warned would precede nuclear escalation – subtle changes in communications patterns, security protocols, and operational procedures that suggested preparation for potential nuclear operations.

"Are we seeing actual weapons movement?"

"Not confirmed, sir. But the patterns are consistent with preparation for elevated readiness rather than normal operations. It could be entirely defensive – protecting their assets in case we escalate further."

"Or it could be preparation for something much worse."

Singh picked up his secure phone to call the Defense Minister. This was information that needed to reach the Prime Minister immediately, but it was also the kind of intelligence that could trigger escalatory responses if misinterpreted.

It was a classic spiral of misperception – each side taking defensive measures that the other saw as offensive preparation, leading to responsive measures that further escalated tensions. The very weapons designed to prevent war were beginning to cast a shadow that might make war more likely.

The stage was set for the most dangerous twelve hours in South Asian history since the Partition of 1947.

The Dream of Fire

May 14, 2025 - 11:00 AM IST

Air Force One, Over the Atlantic

President Trump finally fell into an exhausted sleep, his mind overwhelmed by the complex diplomatic choreography required to prevent nuclear war between two powers whose capabilities had evolved beyond current intelligence assessments. But sleep brought no peace—only a vivid, terrifying dream that would motivate the most urgent diplomatic intervention of his presidency.

In the dream, Trump found himself standing in the Oval Office watching multiple television screens showing breaking news from South Asia. The familiar voices of CNN anchors were reporting something that made his blood run cold:

"This is Wolf Blitzer with breaking news from South Asia. We're receiving reports of what appears to be a nuclear detonation in the Kashmir region. Initial satellite imagery suggests a tactical nuclear weapon has been used in the mountainous area near the Line of Control between India and Pakistan..."

The screen switched to grainy footage of a mushroom cloud rising over mountain peaks, its orange and black plumes spreading across the pristine landscape that had been the site of pilgrimage and prayer for thousands of years. The immediate blast zone was a circle of complete destruction, but the radiation would spread far beyond the initial impact.

Within minutes, the nightmare began escalating beyond South Asia. "This is breaking news," Anderson Cooper's voice cracked with barely controlled panic. "Pakistan has just launched what appears to be a submarine-based nuclear missile toward the Indian naval base at Mumbai. We're receiving reports that India is preparing immediate nuclear retaliation against Karachi and Islamabad."

The screens multiplied, showing simultaneous coverage from around the globe. BBC World Service: "China has just placed its nuclear forces on high alert and is demanding immediate cessation of hostilities. Beijing is threatening nuclear intervention if Pakistani territorial integrity is threatened." RT Moscow: "Russia has activated its strategic nuclear forces in response to what President Putin calls 'an uncontrolled escalation that threatens global security.'"

Trump watched in mounting horror as the localized conflict metastasized into global catastrophe. "Sir," his National Security Advisor said, voice hollow with shock, "we're detecting Chinese nuclear submarines moving toward the Indian Ocean. North Korea has just test-fired three ICBMs over Japan. Iran is mobilizing Revolutionary Guard units. Israel has gone to Defcon 1."

The television screens showed increasingly terrifying images: refugees streaming away from contaminated zones—families carrying children, elderly people collapsing from radiation exposure, mothers clutching dead infants while fleeing poisoned air that would kill everything it touched. But now the refugee streams were global. The ports of Dubai and Singapore were closed due to radioactive fallout carried by monsoon winds. Commercial aviation had ceased worldwide as pilots refused to fly through contaminated airspace.

"Mr. President," the Chairman of the Joint Chiefs explained urgently, "both sides are preparing additional nuclear strikes. Intelligence indicates targeting of major population centers. Mumbai, Delhi, Karachi, Lahore—all under immediate threat. Casualties could reach fifty million in the first hour."

But the nightmare was just beginning. "Sir, we're receiving reports that a Pakistani submarine has been sunk by what appears to be a Chinese torpedo. Pakistan is claiming Chinese betrayal and is threatening Beijing. India is demanding Chinese neutrality but Chinese forces are already engaging Indian aircraft over the Arabian Sea."

The global economic system collapsed in real-time on the screens. "The Dow has fallen 8,000 points in the last hour," CNBC reported. "Global markets are in complete freefall. The dollar is worthless. Oil prices have reached $400 per barrel as the Strait of Hormuz closes due to radiation contamination. Supply chains worldwide have collapsed."

Trump watched European cities—London, Paris, Berlin—where massive crowds surged toward airports and train stations in panic, even though they were thousands of miles from the conflict. "European Union emergency meeting has declared a continental state of emergency," BBC reported. "All borders are closed. Military units are being deployed to prevent refugee influxes from Asia."

The technological infrastructure of civilization began failing. "Cyber attacks are taking down power grids across Asia," a Pentagon briefer reported. "Banking systems in seventeen countries have been compromised. Communications satellites are being jammed or destroyed. We're seeing coordinated attacks on internet infrastructure."

In the dream, Trump took frantic calls from world leaders whose voices reflected the breakdown of international order:

"Mr. President, this is President Macron. France cannot remain neutral if nuclear weapons continue to be used. Our naval forces are being contaminated by radioactive debris in the Indian Ocean. We must intervene militarily."

"Donald, this is Vladimir. Russia will not accept Chinese hegemony in Asia established through nuclear warfare. Our Pacific Fleet is moving to contain the situation. If Chinese forces continue engaging, we will respond appropriately."

"President Trump, this is Prime Minister Kishida. Japan is declaring a national emergency. Radioactive clouds are approaching

our southern islands. We are requesting immediate American military assistance and considering activation of our security partnerships for armed response."

The screens showed the death of globalization in real-time. "International shipping has ceased entirely," reported Sky News. "No vessel will enter the Arabian Sea or Bay of Bengal. Global food supplies are now projected to run out within ninety days. Mass starvation is expected in over forty countries."

Most terrifying were the medical reports flooding in: "Radiation victims are overwhelming hospitals from Dhaka to Bangkok," a WHO spokesperson announced. "We're seeing acute radiation syndrome in over two million people. Medical infrastructure is completely inadequate. International relief organizations cannot reach affected areas due to continued military operations."

Trump watched children in hospitals across South Asia—their hair falling out, their skin burning from invisible radiation, their parents weeping as doctors explained there was no cure, no hope, no escape from the poison that would kill them slowly over weeks. But the suffering was spreading globally as radioactive particles carried by jet streams began contaminating crops in Southeast Asia, poisoning water supplies in Central Asia, creating dead zones that would last for generations.

"Mr. President," the Defense Secretary reported with barely controlled terror, "we're detecting preparations for mass strikes on urban centers. Delhi, Mumbai, Karachi, Lahore, and now Beijing are all being targeted. Chinese nuclear forces are targeting Indian and Pakistani cities in response to attacks on their naval units. We're looking at immediate casualties exceeding one hundred million people."

The final horror came as Trump watched satellite feeds of the world's great cities—New York, London, Tokyo, Moscow—where panic-driven populations fought in the streets for food, water, and any transportation away from urban centers that might become targets. "Civilization as we know it is ending," he thought as he watched the complete breakdown of international law, economic systems, and human society itself.

"Sir," his Communications Director announced with a voice that sounded like the herald of apocalypse, "we're receiving ultimatums. China demands we remain neutral or face nuclear consequences. Russia is threatening strategic strikes if we interfere with their 'peace enforcement operations.' Iran has just declared jihad against all nuclear powers. North Korea is demanding immediate food aid or they will target South Korea and Japan."

The most horrifying aspect was watching millions of innocent people—children playing in parks who would be dead within hours, families eating dinner who would never see tomorrow, students in classrooms who would become radioactive shadows on walls—all completely unaware that human civilization was ending because twenty-three pilgrims had been murdered in a distant mountain valley.

As the dream reached its climax, Trump found himself in the Situation Room watching satellite feeds showing the nuclear destruction of humanity's greatest cities simultaneously: the mushroom clouds over Mumbai and Karachi merged with new clouds over Shanghai and Tehran, while Russian missiles arced toward European capitals in retaliation for NATO's "intervention." The screens showed a planet dying in nuclear fire, two billion people dead or dying, and the survivors facing starvation, disease, and the collapse of everything that had made human civilization possible.

Trump jerked awake in his Air Force One cabin, his heart racing and his body covered in cold sweat. The dream had been so vivid, so detailed, so terrifyingly plausible that for several moments he wasn't sure whether it had actually happened. The images of global nuclear war, dying children on every continent, and the complete collapse of human civilization remained burned into his mind with the clarity of prophetic vision.

He immediately reached for the secure phone, his hands trembling as he realized that preventing the nightmare he had just witnessed was no longer just a diplomatic challenge—it was a desperate race to save human civilization itself from the abyss of nuclear holocaust.

"Get me both Prime Ministers on the line immediately," he told the communications officer, his voice carrying the urgency of a man who had seen the end of the world. " We're going to end this crisis now, before it becomes the catastrophe that destroys everything we've built as a species."

Trump Commands

May 14, 2025 - 2:10 PM

Air Force One, Over the Atlantic

Trump's staff worked frantically to establish secure communications with New Delhi, Islamabad, and key American officials while Air Force One continued its flight toward Washington. The communication technology that allowed the President to coordinate global crisis management from 40,000 feet was about to be tested in preventing nuclear war between powers whose technological capabilities had evolved beyond traditional strategic planning.

Within minutes, Trump was participating in an unprecedented multi-party call that included the leaders of two nuclear powers plus his senior national security team providing real-time intelligence and strategic assessment.

"Gentlemen," Trump began with the authority of someone who had just seen the consequences of failure, "Director Chen is going to brief all of us on current intelligence assessments, because I believe both of you are making decisions based on assumptions that may not reflect the actual strategic situation."

CIA Director Chen's voice came through with professional clarity: "Mr. President, Prime Ministers, our comprehensive assessment indicates that both sides are taking legitimate defensive measures in response to perceived threats, but Pakistani capabilities have evolved significantly beyond Indian intelligence assessments, creating dangerous misperceptions on both sides that could trigger unintended escalation."

"Prime Minister Patel," Trump continued, "I understand you're seeing Pakistani military movements that concern you. Can you describe the Indian response?"

"Mr. President, Pakistan has been positioning armored units for what appears to be preparation for major ground offensive operations while simultaneously demonstrating electronic warfare capabilities that significantly exceeded our intelligence assessments. We have been forced to take appropriate defensive measures to protect our territory and our forces."

"Prime Minister Shah, what's Pakistan's perspective on Indian military activities?"

"Mr. President, India has been massing forces along our border while making obvious preparations at their nuclear facilities that suggest possible escalation beyond conventional means. We cannot ignore such threats to our national survival, particularly given obvious Indian surprise at our legitimate defensive capabilities."

CIA Director Chen interjected with crucial clarification: "Both leaders are describing their own defensive measures accurately, but each side is interpreting the other's defensive actions as preparation for offensive operations. Additionally, Pakistani technological capabilities demonstrated over the past several days appear to have significantly exceeded Indian intelligence assessments, potentially affecting Indian strategic calculations in ways that increase escalation risks."

Trump realized he was listening to two leaders who were both telling the truth as they understood it while being completely wrong about each other's intentions, creating exactly the kind of misunderstanding spiral that had triggered major wars throughout human history. But the technological dimension added dangerous complexity that traditional crisis management approaches might not be able to address.

"Director Chen, explain the technology factor that's complicating this crisis."

"Sir, Chinese technology transfer to Pakistan has created capabilities that approach those of major powers in specific operational domains. Pakistani electronic warfare success against Indian advanced systems, precision artillery performance, and integrated air defense effectiveness all dramatically exceeded previous intelligence assessments by significant margins. This technological surprise may be affecting both sides' confidence in their strategic calculations and their assessment of escalation risks."

The implications were staggering for regional stability and nuclear risk management. Enhanced Pakistani capabilities could theoretically reduce nuclear risks by providing credible conventional deterrence, but they could also increase risks by encouraging Pakistani aggression or by prompting Indian escalation to nuclear levels to overcome unexpected conventional disadvantages.

"Gentlemen, listen to me very carefully," Trump said with the conviction of someone who had seen the alternative. "I'm looking at intelligence that suggests Pakistani defensive capabilities have evolved far beyond what Indian strategic planning anticipated, while Indian forces are taking defensive measures that Pakistan is interpreting as preparation for major offensive operations. This is exactly how nuclear wars start by accident, especially when both sides are operating with strategic assumptions that have been challenged by technological realities and neither side fully understood."

"Mr. President," Prime Minister Patel replied with obvious strain, "Pakistan has demonstrated military capabilities that require us to fundamentally reassess our strategic planning and defensive requirements. We cannot ignore such dramatic technological developments that could affect our national security."

"And India has been taking military measures that strongly suggest they may attempt to escalate beyond conventional means to overcome our enhanced defensive capabilities," Prime Minister Shah responded with equal tension.

Trump felt the full weight of the moment pressing down on him like a physical force. Two nuclear powers, each convinced the other was preparing for war, each operating with strategic assumptions that had been fundamentally challenged by technological realities that neither side completely understood, each moving step by step toward the nuclear threshold that would transform regional conflict into global catastrophe.

"Here's what we're going to do, and I need immediate answers from both of you," Trump said with the absolute authority of the world's most powerful leader who had just seen the consequences of failure. "Both of you are going to issue orders right now—while we're talking—to halt all military movements toward the border. Then we're going to arrange immediate, comprehensive discussions that address not just this immediate crisis but the technological realities that have fundamentally altered regional strategic balance."

"Mr. President," Patel began carefully, "we cannot simply ignore technological developments that have strategic implications for our national security and regional stability."

"And we cannot ignore Indian attempts to negate Pakistani defensive capabilities through escalation to nuclear threats," Shah added with equal firmness.

"Prime Ministers, I'm not asking either of you to ignore anything," Trump replied with growing urgency. "I'm asking you to prevent nuclear war while we all figure out how to manage strategic competition in an environment where technological capabilities have evolved faster than strategic planning and crisis management frameworks. This isn't just about Kashmir anymore, it's about managing strategic stability when technology transfer can rapidly alter regional balances in ways that traditional approaches can't handle."

The secure line fell silent for a long moment that seemed to stretch forever. Trump had just acknowledged that the crisis involved fundamental questions about managing strategic competition in an era of rapid technological change—issues that extended far beyond traditional bilateral dispute resolution into the heart of how major powers would compete in the 21st century.

"I need definitive answers from both of you right now," Trump pressed. "Are you willing to halt military movements immediately and enter into comprehensive discussions about managing strategic stability in the new technological environment? Because the alternative is nuclear war, and that's not acceptable to anyone."

After what felt like an eternity, both leaders agreed to the immediate ceasefire and comprehensive negotiations. But as Trump ended the call, he realized he had just committed the United States to mediating an agreement that would need to account for Chinese technology transfer, Pakistani enhanced capabilities, Indian strategic adaptation, and broader questions about how rapid technological change would affect strategic competition globally.

The immediate nuclear crisis had been averted, but the underlying challenges that had created it remained and would require sustained attention for years to come.

The Announcement

May 14, 2025 - 4:00 PM

Mar-a-Lago, Florida

Trump stood before the assembled cameras in the opulent ballroom of his Florida resort, flanked by American flags and oil paintings of previous presidents, the setting deliberately chosen to project both presidential authority and the personal touch that had characterized his approach to international crisis resolution. The location was highly unconventional for a major diplomatic announcement of this magnitude, but Trump had always preferred to operate outside traditional protocols, and today that unconventional approach had potentially saved human civilization from nuclear catastrophe.

Behind him, his staff scrambled to coordinate with the White House press office, the State Department, the Pentagon, and multiple international partners, most of whom were learning about the comprehensive agreement details for the first time. The unprecedented speed of the crisis had required presidential decision-making that bypassed normal bureaucratic processes entirely, but it had also required acknowledgment of technological realities that challenged fundamental assumptions underlying traditional strategic planning.

"My fellow Americans, and friends around the world," Trump began, looking directly into the cameras with the confidence of a leader who had just prevented nuclear war through personal diplomacy and strategic innovation. "After intensive diplomatic negotiations over the past seventy-two hours that addressed both immediate crisis issues and fundamental long-term strategic stability challenges, I am pleased to announce that India and Pakistan have agreed to an immediate and comprehensive ceasefire that addresses technological realities and strategic competition in entirely new ways."

The announcement sent immediate shockwaves around the world that were visible in real-time through global communication networks. Stock markets that had been plummeting for three days began recovering dramatically. In New Delhi and Islamabad, massive crowds gathered around television screens and mobile devices to hear the details of an agreement that addressed not just the immediate crisis but broader questions about managing strategic competition in an era of rapid technological change that traditional frameworks had not anticipated.

"Both Prime Minister Patel and Prime Minister Shah have demonstrated tremendous leadership, wisdom, and courage in choosing peace over conflict while also acknowledging that technological developments have created new challenges for regional stability that require ongoing attention, cooperation, and innovative approaches to strategic competition."

What Trump was carefully not mentioning publicly was the extraordinarily complex web of technological, economic, strategic, and political issues that had made the agreement possible—Pakistani commitments to comprehensive transparency about Chinese technology assistance, Indian agreement to adapt strategic planning to new technological realities, Chinese acknowledgment of stability concerns created by rapid capability enhancement, and American guarantees of comprehensive support for managing strategic competition through cooperation rather than conflict.

"The comprehensive ceasefire includes several key elements," Trump continued, outlining the agreement's structure. "The immediate return of all prisoners, including the Indian pilot currently in Pakistani custody. A joint investigation into the terrorist attack that initiated this crisis, with international oversight to ensure objectivity. Enhanced counterterrorism cooperation between both countries with American technical assistance. And most importantly, new mechanisms for managing strategic stability in an era where technological change can rapidly alter regional balances in ways that require continuous adaptation."

"The United States has committed to supporting this historic agreement through substantial economic incentives for both countries, enhanced strategic partnerships that address technological competition, ongoing involvement in managing the challenges that modern strategic competition creates for regional stability, and most importantly, sustained attention to preventing future crises that could threaten global security."

Trump was announcing far more than a simple ceasefire—he was unveiling a fundamentally new approach to managing strategic competition in an era where technology transfer could rapidly alter regional balances and where traditional bilateral frameworks were clearly inadequate for complex multi-party strategic relationships involving major powers competing through proxy enhancement.

"This agreement demonstrates that even the most challenging and complex international disputes, complicated by rapid technological change and sophisticated strategic relationships, can be resolved through determined diplomacy rather than devastating warfare. When leaders are willing to put the welfare of their people above narrow political considerations and adapt to new technological realities rather than clinging to outdated assumptions, peace is always possible, even in the most dangerous circumstances."

As Trump concluded his remarks and walked away from the podium, reporters shouted urgent questions about the specific details of the technology provisions, the precise role of Chinese assistance in creating the crisis, the long-term implications for managing strategic competition in an era of rapid technological change, and the broader lessons for international crisis management in the 21st century.

But Trump was already thinking about the much broader implications of what had just been accomplished. The immediate crisis was over, and nuclear war had been prevented, but the technological and strategic realities that had caused the crisis remained and would require sustained international attention. Chinese technology transfer to Pakistan had proven successful in actual combat, potentially encouraging similar relationships in other regions where major powers competed through proxy relationships. Regional strategic balances could be rapidly altered through comprehensive technology provision, requiring entirely new approaches to crisis management and strategic competition.

The agreement had prevented nuclear catastrophe, but it had also acknowledged a new era in strategic competition where technology transfer could rapidly alter capabilities, create new forms of strategic interdependence, and challenge traditional frameworks for understanding alliance relationships, deterrence calculations, and regional stability in the modern era.

Most importantly, the crisis had demonstrated both the enormous risks and the genuine opportunities of technological change in strategic competition, requiring ongoing attention to managing these dynamics responsibly while preventing technological advantages from contributing to rather than deterring dangerous conflicts.

The Global Courtroom

20 May – 28 May 2025

All over the world

Immediately after the ceasefire, India put together several delegations comprising politicians from all parties, including the opposition. These teams visited several countries, telling their leaders that India was right in launching the initial strikes inside Pakistan after the Pahalgam incident. But they found it very difficult going

India's desperate diplomatic campaign was collapsing as leaked intelligence recordings and parliamentary testimony demolished their international credibility.

House of Commons, London

External Affairs Minister Vikram Chandra faced hostile questioning from British MPs who seemed more skeptical than sympathetic about India's retaliatory strikes.

"Minister Chandra," asked the Chairman of the Foreign Affairs Committee, "what specific evidence links the Pakistani state to this terrorist attack?"

"Honorable Chairman, the sophistication of weapons used, the precision of intelligence, the coordination of escape—these indicate state-level support."

"But do you have direct evidence of Pakistani government involvement? Communications intercepts? Financial transfers? Operational orders?"

Chandra felt the room's skepticism. "The circumstantial evidence strongly suggests—"

"Circumstantial evidence, Minister. You've launched military strikes against a sovereign nation based on assumptions rather than proof."

Concurrent - US Congress, Washington D.C.

The all-party Indian delegation faced equally difficult questions from American lawmakers. Congressman Williams from the House Foreign Affairs Committee was particularly pointed:

"Madam Defense Secretary, did India consult with the United States before launching these strikes?"

Defense Secretary Devi tried to maintain composure. "Congressman, India reserves the right to defend itself against terrorism—"

"That's not what I asked. Did you inform your strategic partners before potentially triggering nuclear conflict in South Asia?"

"We informed relevant parties through appropriate channels—"

"After the fact, apparently. How are we supposed to manage global security when allies take unilateral military action without coordination?"

UN Security Council - Emergency Session

The emergency session was devastating for India as even traditional allies distanced themselves from Indian positions.

German Ambassador: "India's own officials have testified that this tragic attack was preventable through improved internal coordination. Military strikes against Pakistan appear to be deflecting from domestic accountability issues rather than addressing legitimate security threats."

French Ambassador: "While we condemn terrorism unequivocally, leaked recordings and parliamentary testimony suggest this crisis stems from institutional failures rather than Pakistani aggression."

Even the American Ambassador seemed uncomfortable: "The United States calls for comprehensive investigation of all factors that enabled this attack before any further military escalation."

Chinese Ambassador Wu Haitao was more direct: "Indian intelligence officials have confirmed that better institutional coordination could have prevented this attack. Military aggression against Pakistan appears designed to cover up domestic failures rather than address legitimate security concerns."

Diplomatic Cables Leaked

By evening, diplomatic cables from various embassies in New Delhi were being leaked, showing private international skepticism:

US Embassy to State Department: *"Indian government appears to be using military action to deflect from serious institutional failures revealed by leaked recordings. Recommend distancing from Indian justifications until comprehensive investigation completed."*

British High Commission to Foreign Office: *"Parliamentary testimony confirms attack was preventable through better Indian coordination. Military strikes appear politically motivated rather than security justified."*

German Embassy to Berlin: *"Indian intelligence failure enabled attack, not Pakistani sophistication. Military escalation seems designed to avoid domestic accountability rather than address terrorism."*

The crisis that began with Pakistani terrorism was increasingly viewed as Indian institutional failure and over-reach, fundamentally altering strategic dynamics and leaving India isolated precisely when they needed international support most.

The Digital War

By evening, the narrative battle was being fought across social media platforms, with professional disinformation campaigns from multiple state actors:

Pakistani narrative: *India launches unprovoked aggression without holding its own errant officials accountable*

Indian narrative: *Pakistan sponsors terrorism then plays victim when held accountable*

Chinese amplification: *Indian military adventurism threatens regional stability*

International skepticism: *Insufficient evidence for military action between nuclear powers*

Aftermath

Jun 4, 2025 - 9:00 AM

Pahalgam, Kashmir

Suresh Sharma, older brother of Ravi who had perished in the terrorist attack that triggered the crisis, stood at the memorial site where the pilgrimage bus had been destroyed just eight days earlier in an attack that had nearly precipitated nuclear war. The burned wreckage had been carefully cleared away by joint Indian-Pakistani teams, but flowers, memorial candles, and photographs of the victims still marked the spot where twenty-three innocent people had died in pursuit of spiritual fulfillment.

But the memorial site now included something unprecedented—a substantial plaque acknowledging the technological and strategic changes that the attack had precipitated, along with commitments from both governments to address the underlying issues that had made such sophisticated terrorism possible. The joint investigation promised by the ceasefire agreement was producing significant results that went far beyond traditional counterterrorism cooperation.

It wasn't simple justice in the traditional sense—the ultimate masterminds of the attack were likely still free, and the underlying political grievances that motivated such violence remained largely unresolved. But it represented a genuine beginning that acknowledged how technological change had fundamentally altered the strategic environment in ways that required new forms of cooperation, intelligence sharing, and coordinated responses to sophisticated threats.

As the sun set over the mountains of Kashmir, casting long shadows across the valley and painting the snow-capped peaks in shades of gold and orange, Suresh placed a final bouquet of flowers on the memorial and reflected on the broader changes that his brother's death had helped precipitate. Ravi and Priya had died in a terrorist attack, but their deaths had also contributed to a crisis that revealed fundamental changes in strategic competition, technology proliferation, and the challenges of maintaining stability in an era of rapid technological change.

The families of all twenty-three victims would receive substantial compensation not just from both governments, but from a broader international fund that acknowledged the global implications of technology-enhanced terrorism and the need for coordinated responses to threats that transcended traditional bilateral relationships. The memorial would serve not just as remembrance of innocent victims, but as recognition of how individual tragedies could catalyze broader strategic adaptations that might prevent future conflicts.

Sometimes, Suresh reflected as he prepared to leave the memorial site, that was the most that could realistically be hoped for from such tragedy—that the dead would not have died entirely in vain, that their sacrifice might contribute to a future where such violence became less likely through better understanding of how technological change affected strategic competition and what international cooperation was required to manage these challenges responsibly.

As he walked back toward his car in the gathering dusk, Suresh noticed something that gave him genuine hope for the future: Indian and Pakistani technical experts were working together at the attack site, jointly examining evidence and developing understanding of how technological enhancement had affected terrorist capabilities and what countermeasures might prove effective. It was a powerful symbol of how crisis could catalyze cooperation that addressed technological challenges requiring joint attention and coordinated responses.

The memorial would stand as a permanent reminder not just of innocent lives lost to senseless violence, but of how technological change could rapidly alter strategic environments in ways that required adaptive cooperation rather than traditional competition. The price of sustainable peace was acknowledgment that strategic competition in the modern era required entirely new approaches that accounted for technological change, technology transfer relationships, and the complex interdependencies that rapid capability evolution created among nations, non-state actors, and the major powers that provided technological assistance.

The future of strategic competition would be significantly shaped by the ability of all parties to understand, adapt to, and manage the implications of technology transfer relationships that could rapidly alter capabilities, create new forms of strategic interdependence, and challenge traditional frameworks for understanding alliance relationships, deterrence calculations, and regional stability in an era of rapid technological change.

The crisis that had begun with twenty-three murdered pilgrims had ended with recognition that the rules of strategic competition had fundamentally changed, requiring new approaches to managing technological competition while preventing such changes from triggering conflicts that could threaten human civilization itself.

The Technical Debrief

Jun 16, 2025 - 10:00 AM

Joint Technical Assessment Center, Chandigarh

The conference room at the hastily established Joint Technical Assessment Center buzzed with the controlled tension of military professionals dissecting one of the most significant intelligence failures in modern South Asian history. Representatives from the Indian Air Force, Pakistani Air Force, Chinese People's Liberation Army, and American technical advisors sat around a horseshoe-shaped table covered with classified documents, satellite imagery, and electronic warfare analysis that would reshape military planning throughout the region.

Air Marshal Vikram Singh, the Indian Air Force's senior technical officer, opened the unprecedented session with the kind of professional honesty that only came after near-catastrophic failure. "Colleagues, we are here because our intelligence assessments were fundamentally incorrect about the technological balance in South Asia. Our pilots flew into an electronic warfare environment that exceeded our worst-case planning assumptions by significant margins."

Across the table, Pakistani Air Commodore Rashid Khan nodded with the satisfaction of someone whose strategic planning had been vindicated in the most dramatic possible way. "Air Marshal Singh, we appreciate your professional candor. Our electronic warfare success was indeed comprehensive, but it was also the result of years of systematic preparation that your intelligence services apparently failed to detect or understand."

The Chinese representative, Colonel Zhang Wei from the PLA's Equipment Development Department, maintained the careful neutrality required for participation in what amounted to a post-conflict technical exchange. His presence alone represented a diplomatic breakthrough, but his technical insights would prove even more valuable for all parties seeking to understand how rapidly regional military balances could be altered through comprehensive technology transfer.

"The integration challenges were substantial," Zhang acknowledged carefully. "Pakistani technical teams demonstrated exceptional proficiency in adapting advanced systems to their specific operational requirements. The learning curve was steeper than conventional arms sales relationships typically require."

American technical advisor Dr. Sarah Mitchell from the Defense Intelligence Agency spread her own analysis across the table. "What we're seeing here represents a fundamental shift in how regional balances can be altered through technology transfer relationships. The speed and comprehensiveness of Pakistani capability enhancement challenges traditional intelligence assessment methods."

Air Marshal Singh reviewed detailed analysis of the electronic warfare engagement that had resulted in Flight Lieutenant Gupta's shootdown. "Our Rafale aircraft were equipped with the SPECTRA electronic warfare suite, considered among the world's most advanced. Yet Pakistani systems achieved systematic degradation of our radar, communications, and navigation systems across multiple aircraft simultaneously."

"The key was integration rather than individual system superiority," Air Commodore Khan explained, displaying technical diagrams that had been declassified for this exchange. "Chinese assistance didn't just provide advanced equipment—it provided comprehensive training in network-centric electronic warfare that enabled coordinated attacks across multiple frequency bands and engagement scenarios."

The implications were staggering for military planning throughout the region. Traditional approaches to capability assessment focused on individual weapons systems and their specifications, but the Pakistani model demonstrated how systematic integration could create overall capabilities that exceeded the sum of individual components.

Dr. Mitchell posed the question that dominated American strategic thinking: "Colonel Zhang, can you describe the replication potential of this integration model? Are we looking at a template that could be applied in other regions facing similar conventional disparities?"

Zhang's response was carefully measured but strategically revealing: "The technical principles are broadly applicable, but successful implementation requires sustained partnership, comprehensive training programs, and most importantly, genuine commitment from all parties to long-term capability development rather than simple arms transactions."

The Chinese officer's emphasis on "sustained partnership" reflected broader strategic logic underlying Beijing's approach to technology transfer—creating lasting relationships that served Chinese interests while providing genuine capabilities enhancement for partners facing conventional pressure from alliance structures.

Indian Navy Captain Priya Sharma, who had observed the crisis from a maritime perspective, raised crucial questions about strategic stability. "The electronic warfare success was indeed comprehensive, but it also created escalation pressures that nearly triggered nuclear exchange. How do we balance capability enhancement with crisis stability when technological surprises can fundamentally alter strategic calculations?"

Air Commodore Khan acknowledged the complexity: "Enhanced conventional capabilities should theoretically reduce nuclear risks by providing credible deterrence through non-nuclear means. But if those capabilities evolve beyond adversary expectations, they can create desperate pressures for escalation that traditional crisis management frameworks cannot handle."

The discussion revealed fundamental challenges for managing strategic competition in an era where technology transfer could rapidly alter regional balances in ways that traditional intelligence assessment and crisis management approaches could not anticipate or control.

Pakistani electronic warfare officer Wing Commander Tariq Ahmed, who had participated in the actual engagements, provided operational insights that would reshape tactical planning: "The real advantage wasn't just technological—it was doctrinal. We developed entirely new approaches to electronic warfare integration that treated the electromagnetic spectrum as a comprehensive battlefield rather than simply defensive enhancement for individual platforms."

American Air Force Colonel James Patterson, reviewing his own service's lessons learned, absorbed implications for global strategic competition: "What you're describing represents a paradigm shift from platform-centric to network-centric electronic warfare. If this approach can be systematically replicated, it could fundamentally alter air combat throughout multiple regions."

The technical debrief continued for three days, with detailed analysis of engagement timelines, electronic warfare techniques, tactical innovations, and most importantly, strategic implications for managing competition in an era where technological advantages could no longer be assumed to be permanent or predictable.

Dr. Mitchell summarized the consensus that emerged: "This crisis has demonstrated that comprehensive technology transfer relationships can rapidly alter regional military balances in ways that traditional assessment methods cannot predict. All parties need enhanced intelligence capabilities, adaptive strategic planning, and crisis management frameworks that account for technological surprise."

But perhaps the most important insight came from Colonel Zhang's closing observations: "Technology transfer succeeds not through equipment provision alone, but through genuine partnership that includes training, integration support, doctrinal development, and sustained technical cooperation. The Pakistani model represents comprehensive capability development rather than traditional arms sales."

As the session concluded, participants understood they had witnessed and analyzed a fundamental shift in how strategic competition would be conducted in the modern era. Technology transfer could rapidly alter regional balances, create new forms of strategic interdependence, and challenge traditional frameworks for understanding alliance relationships, deterrence calculations, and crisis management in ways that would require continuous adaptation by all major powers.

The lessons learned would reshape military planning, intelligence assessment, and strategic doctrine throughout the region and beyond, but they had been purchased at the cost of near-catastrophic nuclear crisis that demonstrated how rapid technological change could outpace strategic wisdom.

One Year Later

May 7, 2026 - 6:15 AM

All over the world

Amarnath Memorial Gardens, Pahalgam, Kashmir

Wing Commander Arjun Singh stood at the memorial dedicated to the twenty-three pilgrims whose deaths had triggered the 72-hour crisis that nearly erupted into nuclear war. The morning air was crisp and clean, filled with the scent of pine and mountain mist, but Singh's perspective on this landscape had been fundamentally altered by events that had reshaped not just his military career, but his understanding of technology, strategy, and human judgment in the modern era.

At 32, Singh now served as the Indian Air Force's senior officer for Electronic Warfare Integration, a position created specifically to address the capability gaps the crisis had revealed. The past year had been a whirlwind of technical adaptation, strategic reassessment, and personal reflection on how rapid technological change could outpace human wisdom.

"Sir," Flight Lieutenant Rahul Gupta approached from behind, his voice carrying the respect of someone whose capture and release had made him a symbol of both technological surprise and diplomatic resolution. Gupta now served as Singh's deputy, their shared experience of Pakistani electronic warfare capabilities making them uniquely qualified to lead Indian adaptation efforts.

The relationship between the two officers had evolved beyond traditional military hierarchy into something approaching genuine partnership forged through shared recognition of how close they had all come to catastrophic failure. Gupta's three days in Pakistani custody had provided insights into adversary capabilities and intentions that formal intelligence gathering had failed to detect.

"Rahul, have you seen the latest assessments from our Chinese counterparts?" Singh asked, reviewing classified documents on a secure tablet that reflected the new era of technical cooperation that had emerged from the crisis.

The memorial service was beginning, with families of the victims gathering around the carefully maintained garden where individual markers honored each person who had died in the attack. But this year's ceremony included something unprecedented—representatives from Pakistan, China, and the United States, acknowledging how the victims' deaths had catalyzed broader strategic adaptations that might prevent future conflicts.

"The Chinese technical exchange has been... illuminating," Gupta replied carefully. "Their willingness to share integration methodologies and training approaches suggests genuine commitment to regional stability rather than simple arms sales relationships."

Singh nodded, reflecting on how his understanding of adversary capabilities and intentions had evolved through sustained professional interaction with the same Chinese advisors who had helped create Pakistani capabilities that had nearly shot him down a year earlier.

The formal memorial ceremony began with speeches from local officials, victim family members, and military representatives from all parties involved in the crisis resolution. But Singh found himself thinking less about the formal proceedings and more about the fundamental questions the crisis had raised about technology, strategy, and human judgment in an era where capabilities could evolve faster than wisdom.

Colonel Mahmood, the Pakistani intelligence officer who had interrogated Gupta during his captivity, was present as part of the joint intelligence cooperation that had emerged from the crisis. His presence represented the kind of professional relationship that had developed between former adversaries who recognized their shared interest in preventing technological advantages from triggering conflicts that could threaten human civilization.

"Wing Commander Singh," Mahmood approached during a break in the formal proceedings, his manner reflecting the professional respect that had developed between military officers on both sides who had participated in near-catastrophic events.

"Colonel Mahmood," Singh replied with the courtesy that characterized their ongoing professional relationship. "I trust the joint electronic warfare exercises have been productive for Pakistani forces as well?"

The question reflected one of the most significant outcomes of the crisis—regular joint training exercises designed to ensure that both sides understood each other's capabilities well enough to prevent future technological surprises from triggering dangerous escalation.

"Extremely productive," Mahmood confirmed. "But more importantly, they've demonstrated that technological superiority isn't permanent or predictable in an era where comprehensive assistance relationships can rapidly alter regional balances."

Their conversation was interrupted by the arrival of Dr. Sarah Mitchell, the American technical advisor who had become a key figure in managing the strategic implications of technology transfer relationships throughout the region. Her presence reflected sustained American engagement in preventing future crises through enhanced understanding of technological competition.

"Gentlemen," she greeted both officers warmly. "The annual assessment is quite encouraging. Electronic warfare incidents along the Line of Control have decreased by 89% since the joint training protocols were implemented."

As the memorial ceremony continued, Singh reflected on how profoundly his worldview had changed through events that had taken him from routine pilot to participant in near-nuclear crisis to architect of new approaches to strategic competition that accounted for rapid technological change.

The families of the victims deserved to know that their loved ones' deaths had contributed to strategic adaptations that might prevent future tragedies, but they also deserved honest acknowledgment that technological competition would continue in new forms that required constant vigilance and adaptive cooperation.

"Sir," Gupta observed quietly, "do you think we've genuinely learned the lessons this crisis was trying to teach us?"

Singh considered the question with the seriousness it deserved, thinking about technological developments already emerging that could create new forms of strategic surprise and competitive pressure. "Rahul, I think we've learned that technological superiority is temporary, that intelligence assessments can be fundamentally wrong, and that strategic competition requires ongoing adaptation rather than assumptions based on historical precedent."

Concurrent - May 7, 2026

Strategic Forces Command, Islamabad

General Tariq Baig stood in the same underground command center where he had contemplated nuclear escalation a year earlier, but now his focus was on managing strategic competition in ways that enhanced rather than threatened regional stability. The electronic status boards still displayed Pakistan's nuclear arsenal, but they also showed new systems for crisis communication, joint training coordination, and technological cooperation that had emerged from near-catastrophic failure.

At 59, Baig had become one of the leading advocates for nuclear risk reduction through enhanced conventional capabilities and sustained strategic dialogue. His experience during the 72-hour crisis had convinced him that nuclear weapons were too dangerous for deterrence strategies that relied on crisis escalation and mutual fear.

"General," his aide announced, "the annual strategic assessment is ready for your review."

The assessment represented one of the most significant innovations to emerge from the crisis—comprehensive, joint evaluation of regional strategic balance that included input from all major stakeholders and focused on preventing technological surprises from creating dangerous misperceptions.

Baig reviewed key findings that reflected fundamental changes in how strategic competition was being managed throughout South Asia:

- Electronic warfare capabilities had become symmetrical through sustained technical cooperation, reducing potential for technological surprise

- Joint training exercises had created mutual understanding of capabilities that prevented misperception-driven escalation

- Crisis communication mechanisms had been tested through regular exercises that simulated various escalation scenarios

- Intelligence sharing had identified emerging technological developments before they could create strategic surprise

But the assessment also identified continuing challenges that required ongoing attention:

- Chinese technology transfer relationships were expanding globally, potentially creating similar capability shifts in other regions

- Rapid technological change continued to outpace strategic planning cycles, requiring enhanced adaptive capacity
- Domestic political pressures in both countries still favored aggressive responses to perceived technological disadvantages
- Alliance relationships and great power competition created pressures for technological development that could destabilize regional balance

"The most significant finding," Baig told his senior staff, "is that strategic stability requires ongoing adaptation rather than static balance. The moment we assume we understand the technological environment is the moment we become vulnerable to strategic surprise."

The observation reflected broader lessons learned about managing strategic competition in an era where technological change could rapidly alter capabilities, create new forms of strategic interdependence, and challenge traditional frameworks for understanding alliance relationships and deterrence calculations.

Concurrent - May 7, 2026

Beijing Command Center

General Liu Wei reviewed global strategic assessments that reflected how the Pakistani model of technology transfer had been adapted and replicated throughout multiple regions where China sought to alter balance dynamics through comprehensive assistance relationships. The success of Chinese electronic warfare systems in actual combat had validated strategic approaches to technology proliferation that were reshaping global strategic competition.

But Liu was also studying reports that reflected unintended consequences of technological success that required careful management to prevent destabilization rather than enhanced deterrence.

"Comrade General," his deputy reported, "the annual assessment indicates successful replication of the Pakistani integration model in four additional regions, but it also identifies escalation risks in two theaters where rapid capability enhancement exceeded adversary expectations."

The reports reflected fundamental challenges of managing technology transfer relationships that served Chinese strategic interests while maintaining regional stability. Enhanced capabilities could increase deterrence and reduce conflict risks, but they could also create desperate pressures for escalation if they exceeded adversary planning assumptions.

Liu studied detailed analysis of strategic outcomes in regions where Chinese technology transfer had been implemented:

- Southeast Asia: Enhanced air defense capabilities had deterred alliance intervention but had also triggered military modernization that increased overall regional tensions

- Middle East: Advanced missile systems had strengthened partner deterrence but had also prompted adversary development of countermeasures that could destabilize broader regional balance

- Africa: Electronic warfare capabilities had prevented external intervention but had also created dependencies that could draw China into local conflicts

- Latin America: Naval systems had enhanced coastal defense but had also triggered American security concerns that complicated broader strategic relationships

"The fundamental challenge," Liu concluded, "is that technological success creates both opportunities and obligations that traditional strategic planning frameworks cannot adequately address."

The insight reflected broader questions about managing strategic competition in an era where technology transfer could rapidly alter regional balances while creating new forms of strategic interdependence that affected crisis management, alliance relationships, and great power competition in ways that traditional approaches could not anticipate or control.

Epilogue: The Watchers

May 7, 2028 - Three Years Later

Undisclosed Location

The encrypted hard drive arrived at the investigative journalist's office in Geneva via untraceable courier, just as similar drives had reached select recipients in Washington, Beijing, and London over the past month. No return address. No digital fingerprints. Only a single folder labeled "Pahalgam - The Truth."

Inside the folder, financial transaction records spanning three years. Shell companies in seven countries. Cryptocurrency transfers totaling $50 million. Training facility rentals in remote locations. Equipment purchases from multiple suppliers. Communications intercepts in languages that included neither Urdu nor Hindi.

The most disturbing document was a strategy memo, meticulously detailed but bearing no organizational letterhead or signature:

"Operation Catalyst - Phase 1 Complete. Indian-Pakistani military confrontation achieved as projected. Enhanced Chinese-Pakistani cooperation and Indian strategic adaptation proceeding according to scenario planning. Media subversion successfully tested.

American diplomatic intervention successful in preventing nuclear escalation while establishing new crisis management frameworks that serve long-term strategic objectives..."

The memo continued with clinical analysis of how the Pahalgam attack had achieved multiple strategic goals: validating Chinese military technology in combat conditions, forcing comprehensive review of Indian intelligence institutions, establishing American-mediated regional stability frameworks, and creating precedents for managing technology transfer relationships globally.

But it was the final paragraph that made the journalist's hands tremble:

"Phase 2 preparations should commence following three-year stabilization period. Recommended target: Southeast Asian scenario utilizing enhanced capabilities demonstrated in South Asian proof-of-concept. Estimated probability of limited nuclear exchange: 12%. Acceptable risk parameters for advancing global strategic architecture goals..."

Twenty-three innocent pilgrims. Two nuclear powers brought to the brink of war. Global strategic frameworks fundamentally altered. All of it apparently orchestrated by unknown actors whose identity remained hidden behind layers of financial obfuscation and operational compartmentalization.

The journalist stared at the documents, understanding that the 72-hour war might have been neither Indian incompetence nor Pakistani terrorism, but something far more sinister—a carefully managed crisis designed to reshape global strategic competition while testing the limits of nuclear brinkmanship.

In the growing darkness outside his office window, the journalist wondered: if Pahalgam had been a test, what was the actual plan?

And somewhere in the shadows of the modern world, the watchers continued their patient work.

About the author

Alok Asthana is a retired Col of the Indian army. He served 26 years in the Indian infantry – 4/4 GR and 8 RR, the unit he raised in 1994. He also served two tenures as an instructor at the Infantry School, and one at the Senior Command Wing of the Army War College. He is now a military analyst, with several publications.

He has studied this topic extensively and written three books on it – each with a different twist, for a different reader. The first two books provide the data and reasons. The first book on it – **Op Sindoor – Force Multipliers and Dividers: What worked and what did not** – is a data-driven technical analysis where data is presented mostly in the form of tables with some explanations. The researcher will find it invaluable. The other book – **Strategic leverage; The novel about how Op Sindoor got checkmated** – presents the facts that gave rise to the data, but as dialogues between diplomats, former generals, intelligence officers, and journalists from across South Asia, participating in a 3 day seminar. much after the war. That format greatly facilitates assimilation of facts. This third book is a proper novel. It is not at all about data, but the story.

Col A Asthana stays at Thane, India. He can be contacted at alok.asthana@gmail.com

Also by

- **Handing down Battle-tested leadership Practices: From the War room to the Board room** – The leadership book, complete with theories and case studies.
- **Alok's Field Guide on Leadership: 42 Leadership Techniques from the War room to the Board room** – Crystallized from the book above, 42 actionable techniques for team leadership, each a gold mine.
- **Reclaim your Democracy** – Techniques to reclaim democracy, where ever you live.
- **Beat Chronic Diseases** – A primer on how diet, particularly carbs, affect our health.
- **The Red Pill on India and the Indian Army 2023: See them as they really are**
- **The 7 Fault Lines of the Indian Army – India's own 'Crisis in Command' and 'Psychology of Military Incompetence'**
- **The Geometry of Wild Flowers** – A novel about a Questioning man

- **Op Sindoor- Force multipliers and dividers: What worked and what did not.**

- **Strategic Leverage – The novel on how Op Sindoor got checkmated.**

9 789334 352115

Printed at Repro India Ltd.